PIECES OF A PATTERN

PIECES OF A PATTERN

LACROIX
by Christian Lacroix

Edited and Introduced by
Patrick Mauriès

With over 260 illustrations,
134 in colour

THAMES AND HUDSON

Any copy of this book
issued by the publisher as a paperback is sold subject to the
condition that it shall not by way of trade or otherwise be
lent, resold, hired out or otherwise circulated without the
publisher's prior consent in any form of binding or cover
other than that in which it is published and without a similar
condition including these words being imposed on a
subsequent purchaser.

Translated from the French by Barbara Mellor

Introduction © 1992 Patrick Mauriès
Text © 1992 Christian Lacroix
Layout © 1992 Christian Lacroix and Thames and Hudson Ltd, London

Printed and bound in Japan

CONTENTS

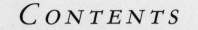

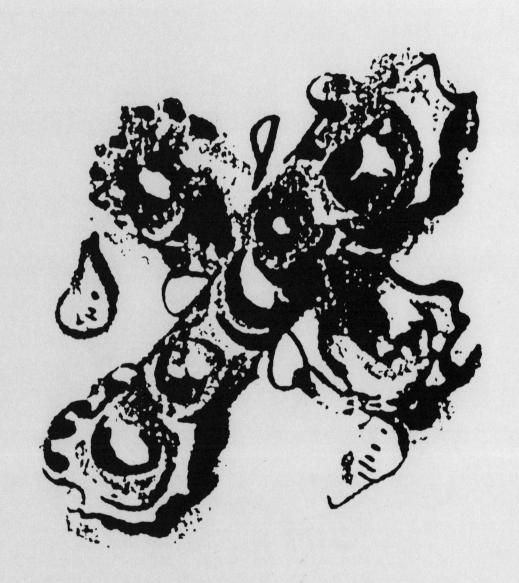

A CHILD OF THE MIDI

by Patrick Mauriès

*I*n these times, so intent on naming, labelling and analysing, when the 'look' of a particular fashion designer is no longer simply a question of proportions or of the relationship of length to volume but has to express some social phenomenon; in these times when fashion design is seen as a matter of symptoms and interpretation, what can the name Lacroix be taken to signify?

Let us try to recall (not without some difficulty five years on, so quickly do philosophies of fashion come and go) the background against which his earliest creations, or his first public images at least, made their appearance. The fashion world was then living out the myth of its own destruction, a myth, incidentally, that was to prove as brief as it was intense. The Japanese had erupted suddenly upon the scene, as though charged with a mission to reveal to the West the truth about its own futility – a truth that was to last all of three or four seasons. River-washed fabrics, coarse-woven wools, linens knotted and slashed; a colour spectrum ranging from anthracite through ash grey to smoky black; a minimalism fit for Armageddon, the menace of the atomic age in microcosm, a frenzied puritanism – enough deliciously punitive motifs, in fact, to plunge fashion editors with shudders of delight into a world of self-mortifying terrorism. To this were added distant echoes of 'impoverished' street culture, the destructive playfulness of the aptly named World's End, the flamboyance of Vivienne Westwood and Malcolm McLaren, and an element of that cultural anarchy which only the English know how to carry off.

It was at this point that there appeared on the scene a sensualist, addicted to fabrics, captivated by different materials and motifs, aware of the history of fashion, but without being either slavishly obsessed with it or affecting a sort of counter-culturalist amnesia, as if there were no past beyond twenty years ago: a sensualist, in short, quite simply and straightforwardly happy with his lot.

His reputation had of course gone before him; his name was already well known among the 'happy few' who hurried to Hermès and Patou, jostling for elbow-room in salons that before had either been virtually deserted or reserved for a handful of clients who were themselves *passé*. Now, overnight, all the apocalypses in chiffon, the millennial muslins, the prophetic rendings and the makeshift asceticism were forgotten. Here, re-emerging in all its splendour, was the time-honoured mythology of fashion, with all its improbable excesses and scandalous, unjustifiable profligacy. Dedicated wholeheartedly to satisfying his own cravings, this sensualist gave new life to rustling and long-forgotten materials, to paddings and hairpieces, to poufs – those famous poufs – and a fullness of fabric worthy of Dior, to deceptive corsages and fichus; in short, to a whole vocabulary of fashion which – as will be seen later – press and public lost no time in linking with the mythology of the eighteenth century.

The fashion world was itself enjoying a tremendous vogue at the time, of course, with people rushing from show to show in order to celebrate, at considerable expense, the glory of the 'creators'. But the accent was beyond doubt on the 'lay' branch of the sacred vocation, that is, on the rapidly expanding ready-to-wear market, and also on the universal cult of narcissism, fostered to cater to a particular brand of American sociology. It was impossible to keep count of the new labels and personalities appearing out of nowhere, riding on the crest of the wave of popular culture. A product of his times, Lacroix – who still today enjoys visiting the most insignificant showroom, melting happily into the enthusiastically curious crowd – was perfectly well aware of all this. But – and perhaps for that very reason – he chose instead to return to that 'other' mythology and to offer a prolonged reprieve to a magnificently exuberant, ruinously expensive and old-fashioned 'couture', with its painstaking techniques and inordinately demanding levels of skill. Himself a sign of his times as much as an interpreter of them, Lacroix was unaware that he was to fulfil a multitude of desires and give expression to many long-unspoken needs, now rising again to the surface.

In their way the 'devastated' fashions of 1979–80 were another indication of the tiredness of the modernist canon, of the cult of economy – so mechanical, so easy – of the equation of form and function, of harsh contrasts, and of the unrelenting insistence on purity and simplicity. At the same time, an awareness that frenetic modernism could well be a mask for conformity did not necessarily entail an unthinking acceptance of the simple inversions of post-modernism, with its veneerings and collagism, its negative irony, and its passionate determination to reject everything that had gone before. No: what was needed was to find another way, to start from a different assessment of the present, to lay oneself open to a world of shapes and colours, neither rejecting the past nor alluding to it superficially. It was time for a new mythology.

So much then for the image of the Lacroix label, which arguably finishes at the point where the designer's true world begins – a world composed of different elements which need to be isolated and analysed. The eighteenth-century Lacroix, mesmerized by hoops and paddings and thrust so insistently before our eyes, is one element. This side of Lacroix – which exists, of course, and which can be glimpsed in any number of asides and quotations – can be traced back to the young devotee of fashion who wanted to become a costume historian before he turned to matters of more account. But few people have taken into consideration the fact that this is an eighteenth century that has been viewed through a double filter, so to speak. For Lacroix's vision of the eighteenth century, as in a Chinese morality tale, was based on someone else's dream: his inspiration owes less to the courtly, formal world of Versailles than to the more bourgeois and whimsical world of the Second Empire, with its rosettes and panniers brought back into fashion by a nostalgic empress indulging her dreams of creating a court resembling a bucolic utopia. And even then, the Second Empire which fascinated Lacroix – this world of pastoral excursions and seductions, with the old order and an outmoded way of life expiring gracefully, with only a hint of bitterness, among a froth of pretty little rituals – was submitted to a second filtering process.

His first introduction to this world was through the pages of those bundles of old copies of *L'Illustration* or *Le Magasin pittoresque* with which every genteel French attic was crammed in the 1950s. More important, however, were his memories of the films of Ophüls and of a particular brand of French cinema of the time, of *Madame de . . .* and *Lola Montez*, and of the portrait they painted, at once sumptuous and bittersweet, of a society where all was wit and frivolity, where elegance was merely the reverse side of modesty, emotion of repartee, and whose consummate sophistication was unable to conceal a hint of despair; a world in which laces and taffetas served to smother – or to encase – doomed passions and delirious raptures, forbidden and fanned by a strict sense of duty and propriety.

The same is true of Lacroix's alleged ornamentalism, so quick to provoke righteous indignation among critics given to cut-and-dried judgments, who in the absence of any true aesthetic rationale in this domain tend to condemn his work as 'decorative'. Lacroix's taste for ornament, rooted as it is in his temperament and his personal background, is informed by historical influences at the same time as being an expression of his determination to breach the traditional opposition of town and theatre, of everyday garments and furnishing fabrics, of clothes for show and clothes for ordinary life. Not for him the negative irony and criticism of post-modernism; in his view the function of design is to delve deep into the realm of memory, and so to become part of an overall vision.

Similarly, the constant reference to Arles in Lacroix's work would soon have become irritating were it not for the fact that it springs from a sort of family epic, a personal myth which he feels a constant compulsion to take apart and put back together again, like an enigmatic jigsaw puzzle whose overall design can never quite be grasped.

Without falling back on the ambiguous and overworked notion of authenticity, it is quite legitimate to claim that part of Lacroix's success is due to the perfectly judged tone of the myth that he has woven around himself. Coming as he did from a region full of light, colour and openness, he struck a chord with a society hankering increasingly for the gentle pleasures of life, and for symbols of sunshine and the warm south – a craving expressed in countless ways in contemporary decoration and fashion as well as in the press. But, it has to be said, it could all have been simply a matter of luck.

Such constant recourse to personal imagery could well have been a hindrance rather than a help to Lacroix's career. What is so intriguing about his approach is the way in which he has been able to marshall all the different elements that make up the world of his imagination and share them with a tremendously varied public. So much so that he has been awarded the supreme distinction of appearing on the cover of *Time* magazine, an accolade which generally speaking gives the recipient the right to claim the grandiose title of 'fashion designer of his generation'. Whatever the case, fashion designer of *a* generation, however limited it may be, Lacroix certainly is. Born bang in the middle of the century and arriving in Paris in the 1970s, eager to see everything and fascinated by all that was going on in the worlds of painting, fashion, cinema and theatre, he was indelibly marked by everything those years had to offer.

And from the outside – that is, from the lofty vantage point of the twenty years that separate us from that seminal period – how is it possible for anyone to imagine the importance for this young man from the south, among others, of the perfect face, pale, mask-like and haunting, of some forgotten model acting badly in an Andy Warhol film? Or early issues of *Interview*, which could only be found in one particular shop in the boulevard Saint-Germain? Or the inexhaustible delights yielded by a slim, obscure volume by Philippe Jullian, a sort of iconoclastic history of decoration? Or the charm of Hammer horror films, with their Victorian settings, their rain-washed landscapes and their cardboard manor houses? Or the fascination of the stylized world and diaphanous elegance of a Cecil Beaton, and the graphic perfection of the Ascot scene from *My Fair Lady*? Or the luminous, spirited beauty of a Danielle Darrieux? Or the impact of Patrice Chéreau's production of Marivaux's *La Dispute*, with its menacing shadows and fragile characters? Or the feelings of delight provoked by the sight of a monkey-like actress, shimmering with sequins and paste, delivering an acid commentary in a South American accent on scenes from a Parisian casino, taking place around a monumental ceremonial staircase (*Luxe* by the TSE group)? Or a handful of hysterics, hatted and plastered with make-up, uttering eagle-like shrieks as they mingled with the audience in the basement at Le Palace (Copi's *Les Quatre Jumelles*)? A time of immense freedom, of sudden opening up on all sides, of unbridled theatricality, of game-playing and improvisation, and of cross-fertilization at every level, it also saw the last films of Pasolini and Visconti, as well as *More* and *Fellini Satyricon*. And it was at this time too that fashion began rapidly to assume the importance that it still has today, and that our image of the human body was transformed.

So there it is, a jumble of odds and ends, a loose inventory which will be familiar to anyone who lived through that time, and whose influence on Lacroix, as he himself emphasizes, was profound. There is nothing here, naturally, which is indispensable to an 'understanding' of his work, but these few clues may help in tracing it back to its true roots, in freeing it from the superficial impulses which people tend to impute to it, and, if nothing else at least, in recognizing its points of departure and measuring the distance it has covered. It is a distance, and an achievement, that assumes all the more significance in the case of someone who is remarkable for the unqualified trust that he displays in his dealings with other people and in all that life scatters in his path: the strokes of luck and the hazards of destiny, the enthusiasms and, ultimately, the evolution of a passion. And it is to an exploration of that passion that this book invites us.

was born there, but on the other bank of the Rhone, in a village called Trinquetaille. It was a village that had suffered particularly badly in the bombardments of August 1944, and the scars were still visible during my childhood: my route to school was lined with surviving stumps of blackened wall, patchworks of old wallpaper, and bits of paving stones and mosaics. An entire, gentle way of life seemed to have vanished, to be replaced by a melancholy jumble of chaotic reconstruction work, narrow streets of bargees' houses, miraculously left unscathed, with their façades limewashed in different colours, and a few substantial and rather dreary middle-class houses from the nineteenth century.

For me Trinquetaille meant school, with desks black with age and scored with graffiti left as mementoes of their passing by former generations – possibly indeed our fathers or grandfathers. A coal stove was enclosed by iron bars, and the walls were painted cream above and dark brown below. Children who lived in farmhouses in the Camargue would come to school in the traditional black cotton smocks with red trim and buttons; the more urbane ones like myself, of the *Mon Oncle* generation, used to wear a shorter, all-enveloping garment in pink or blue gingham, unbelted and sometimes

A nursery schoolmate.

embroidered. In the harsh southern winters the girls from the country wore flannel trousers gathered at the ankle under their kilts. With their hair cut square or tied in plaits round their heads, the more modern among them sporting boys' haircuts or ponytails, they had a slightly military air, like army canteen ladies, which rather appealed to me. I meanwhile had to endure having my hair shorn like a G.I.: the bald barber would screw up his eyes against my springy locks, which used to fly into his face as he cut them, muttering in his Spanish accent and not without a touch of envy, 'Just like boars' bristles, just like boars' bristles'. His salon, in Henri II style, was painted in blood-red and gold, possibly in homage to his native land – or was it an attempt at modernism?

My mother in the early 1950s.

My mother had adopted the rather effective 'sporty' elegance that was so characteristic of that time. In winter she would wear a long beige or russet coat with enormous buttons, knitted twinsets, white blouses, straight skirts, a beret and suede or lizardskin shoes. Summer was more conventional, with full sunray-pleated skirts in Provençal prints, pink gingham worn with a gold belt, grey cambric and broderie anglaise.

Trinquetaille also meant the cemetery, where the oldest monuments had carved marble books propped up on top of them, embellished with enamelled medallions bearing portraits of the dead. These photographs in their daguerrotype tones fascinated me: *Arlésiennes* wearing long ribbons in 1880s fashion; Camargue cowboys sporting sideburns; young girls crowned with the bouffant curls of the 1920s; languid young fops, their hair glistening with brilliantine; profiles from the 1940s; children in sailor suits; an entire family of strangers, suddenly so familiar. In those days funeral wreaths were made from thousands of tiny pearls in shades of mauve and blue, fashioned into sprays of flowers or abstract, geometric arabesques. There was one grave that always appealed to me particularly: sitting on top of it, sculpted life-size, were three old ladies chatting in the Provençal dialect: 'What are you thinking about?' 'About our death.'

Trinquetaille also meant my great-grandmother and some of her family, installed in a vast walled garden which had been part of an eighteenth-century glassworks. Nothing there seemed to have changed much since the nineteenth century, certainly not the wide-brimmed varnished cloth hat that she wore tied under her chin in summer, nor the infinite variety of different shades of black that she used to wear – 'flea' black, 'bull' black, midnight black, ink black – relieved only by a frugal scattering of stitching or pattern in white.

Finally, and above all, Trinquetaille meant my father's family, who all lived together in an apartment building that had escaped the bombing, with terrace balconies and balustrades. Life there revolved around the workshops, offices and shops of an agricultural machinery business, with the latest, most advanced American machinery displayed, like so many dinosaurs in fire-engine red and brilliant yellow, among a forest of plants. The red-brick workshop with its glass roof painted stained-glass blue was as deafening inside as the forge of the Cyclops. The living quarters were reached through the offices, filled with an assortment of furniture in different styles – traditional Provençal, Third Republic and 1940s.

My great-grandmother, as I remember her.

Sixties fashion.

The elegance of the women who surrounded me had an almost tribal quality. It went beyond the fashion of the day, which they used to adapt to their own clearly defined style in ways that were as timeless and unchanging as they were particular to themselves: immaculately piled up hair; organdie or satin blouses, invariably long-sleeved; dark twill suits or shirt-dresses; gleaming black pumps or sandals; and strings of grey pearls. The discreet range of colours was never extended beyond four different shades, the only violation of this unwritten code being their impeccably manicured long red fingernails. These were always dried by blowing on them while moving the fingers together from side to side: a tacit and carefully choreographed ritual which served to reaffirm their membership of the clan.

My grandmother so worshipped white that for his first communion my
father, who had red hair and pale skin, was forced to wear a spotlessly white
Eton suit. My mother for her part consigned me to the colour red – most
notably a red velvet cape of which I was particularly proud, as I had heard
people compare me when I was wearing it to Gérard Philipe in his costume
for *Le Cid* at Avignon.

Only one of these women, distant and mysterious, seemed to take pleasure in
flouting this grey/white/black/beige tradition. There can be no doubt that it
was the influence of her scarlet suits, her stiletto heels, her panther toques and
collars, her make-up in shades of bronze, her enormous earrings and her
crisp, short hairstyles that made me understand what fashion really was: an
elegance that makes itself noticed.

My father on the day of his
first communion.

o there was Trinquetaille, lying in the delta
between the Rhone and the Petit Rhone, with its
school and homework, and all the little obligations of childhood. Our house stood at the
crossroads of the roads to Nîmes, the Cévennes
(where this gentle, strict, kind and formidable
family had its origins), the Camargue, Les Saintes-Maries-de-la-Mer, and
finally Arles. We used to come upon the most beautiful view of the town
during dangerously seductive walks on the opposite bank of the river:
crenellated with towers and belfries in white stone, it lay before us like some
giant jaw-bone bleached and dried by the sun. Arles was a different story
altogether, another side to life: Arles meant Thursdays and Sundays, the
other family, a different century – and Provence.

In order to reach Arles a bridge had to be crossed, both literally and
metaphorically, for it meant leaving behind my father's world and moving
into my mother's, complementary but different; wrapped up well against the
mistral, I always felt a sense of adventure when we crossed to the other side of
the river.

Before the war my maternal grandparents used to live close to the bridge, in a building that had once been a seminary, complete with a belfry in the form of a cupola. When it threatened to collapse in the wake of the blast caused by the bombing, they moved to a house that seemed to me to be a labyrinth of rooms with red tiles, flowery wallpaper or whitewashed walls. Up above were a terrace and the attic, where I was to discover hidden treasure: bound volumes of *La Mode illustrée* of 1860, which probably would have meant nothing to anybody else and were therefore evidently intended for me, together with all the wherewithal for dressing up. It is perfectly possible that I owe my fondness for salmon pink to a shabby ballgown in wartime material, and my taste for chocolatey purple to another in Moroccan crepe, both of which I found abandoned up there.

On the ground floor were a shop and workshop, a pungent empire of leather, grease and wax belonging to a saddler and his wife, who became rather like supplementary grandparents to me. The front of the shop was festooned with hundreds of little bells destined for the herds that still used to be driven through Arles in the early morning when I was a child. Inside, perched on trestles, were saddles for cowherds – stuffed, cushioned, padded and covered with brown and beige checked material edged in red, unchanged since the Renaissance. And hanging from the ceiling were the skins of bulls and horses, white, black or dappled.

My mother used to ask them to make belts for us from plaited horsehair, with leather buckles in the form of tridents or horseshoes. The Emperor Bao-Dai used to send in his revolver holsters to be repaired, and Cocteau would spend hours at a time there discussing the subject of Craftsmanship considered as an Art. I was undoubtedly busy all the while collecting impressions and storing up sensations for future use. Though I had already discovered television at Trinquetaille with the marriage of Prince Rainier and Princess Grace of Monaco, my Thursdays in Arles were always spent in the saddlery.

I should perhaps say something about the television of those years: after the Rin Tin Tin cartoons I was allowed to watch *Le Magazine féminin*, a programme of the lapdogs-and-candelabra variety presented by Maïté Célérier de Sanois, which featured the latest Paris fashions, sketched somewhat vaguely by the designers themselves. The final item was a course in cutting out, given by a woman with Russian-looking cheekbones with a model behind her wearing an extremely demure waspie, in whose presence I was nevertheless always told to shut my eyes, a piece of advice which I never followed.

The true god of my childhood world in Arles was my grandfather. Just as the women of my father's family were the high priestesses of the Trinquetaille matriarchy, so my grandfather was the undisputed and indisputable god on the opposite bank of the Rhone. A patriarch of consummate elegance in the manner of Jules Berry, he had asked his tailor several years before his death to make the morning suit in which he wished to be buried. His wife, meanwhile, despite a fine Bourbon profile and the loveliest skin that I have ever seen outside the British royal family, took not the slightest interest in her appearance. Together they made a strangely ill-assorted couple, one of those incongruous yet inseparable alliances which families tended to enter into in those days, and which were not necessarily as bad a thing as they might have seemed. My father shared the elegance of his father-in-law: as a teenage refugee in the Cévennes during the German occupation he had written to his parents to inform them that he wanted his next season's suit to be 'Crazy, *parbleu*!'. At his tailor's, the walls were decorated all round with a frieze painted by Léo Lelée showing the history of the suit in sufficient detail to set me daydreaming – or at least it would have done, had it not been for the crossbred bulldog which used to emit squeaks rather than barks when you pulled on its chain. While all this was going on my father would be sucking on his pipe as he tried on tweed jackets, suede waistcoats and checked shirts with English collars.

My father derived a pleasure that was as touching as it was naive in reproducing faithfully the images in Léo Lelée's paintings. The people of

Provence hold this great painter of the traditional dress of Arles in the same high esteem as the poet Mistral and the Marquis de Baroncelli, leaders of the *félibrige* movement, the aim of which was to preserve the Provençal dialect. They recognize themselves in his faithful observation of the folds of a shawl, of the traditional *farandole* dances, of typical Provençal postures and attitudes, of the infinitely varied features of the people of Arles, their movements and bearing, and of the beauty of the colours of the place and its inhabitants. It goes without saying that I too used to imitate and admire Lelée's work, especially his drawings of bulls, of horses, and of everything, great or small, to do with the corrida.

inked forever in my mind with Arles, as it is for many others who admire the place as whole-heartedly as I do, is a shrine which I prefer even above the church of Saint-Trophime: the Muséon Arlaten, the town's true shrine, with its Christmas cribs made out of bread, its amulets and religious relics, its local Tarascon dragon, its stuffed animals, its diorama showing a lying-in room from the turn of the century, and its costume belonging to that goddess of the 1940s, Rejoneadora Conchita Cintron, the south's most famous female bullfighter – in short, a sublime time machine, turning back the clock of everyday life. We used to walk there nearly every Thursday, passing on our way, in no particular order: the lions of the Hôtel de Ville; the blind man and the paralysed man on the Archbishop's Palace; the Florentine mansion of the Marquis de Luppe; the gypsy encampment beside the canal; the winter garden, laid out *à la française*; the rue Parade with its seven bends; the theatre covered with masks in pink plush; the nuns in their pointed white coifs; young girls making their first communion in organdie dresses and veils, paying visits all round the town with their hatted and gloved mothers throughout the month of May; their male counterparts in white armbands; the Berniniesque barley-sugar columns of the rue de la République; the circuses and travelling fairs on the place de la Croisière; the trophies made of feathers, chocolate ribbons and crystallized fruits which we used to dedicate to Saint-Césaire on Palm Sunday; the bas-relief portrait of Julius Caesar on the façade of the hotel named after him; and the strange architecture of the Turkish baths on the bank of the Rhone.

The itinerary of my adolescence used to proceed from college to the Café Malarte on the Lices (smoke-filled and noisy, with plants dotted around among wicker chairs, occupied on one side of the room by the 'bourgeois' drinking tea, and on the other by the 'dandies' affecting a superior air) by way of the Musée Réattu. Its mullioned windows, overlooking a bend in the river, receive the full force of the mistral and of the greenish waves that it whips up. This is a place of homage to the Atelier de Couture and to Raspal's portraits, to Picasso and to Zadkine. In summer there was Verdi, Bizet or Gounod in the Roman theatre, dazzling sunshine, melting tar, and not a breath of air. There was also the corrida and – highlight of the year – the festival of costume on the first Sunday of July, with fisherwomen from Marseilles and *Arlésiennes* in the fashions of Napoleon III, the eighteenth-century or the Louis Philippe era, all parading before the Queen of the Festival, who was always on horseback and dressed in white.

Myself on Palm Sunday in the 1950s.

Arles meant a world of artifice and the baroque, of gentle and civilized folly and solemn futility. 'The people here are much more artistic than in the North, both in their features, so characteristic of the region, and in the way they live their lives,' wrote Vincent van Gogh to his brother Theo from Arles. He was describing an impression, the truth of which he was uniquely qualified to judge, having suffered so greatly on account of it. And never is art so much part of life in Arles as on the days of the corrida.

Léo Lelée (*left*) mixed the Arles farandole with the style of a Greek vase. My father admired his work so much that he copied or redrew many of his paintings.

Left This is a perfect example of Arles beauty, a profile close to the Greek ideal. The shawl is all pinned, never sewn. It is a late 1940s/ early 1950s costume, which is why no hat ribbon can be seen. At the turn of the century the ribbon reached the shoulders and that is the style that is usually adopted today.

The costumes of the Arles region have had a deep influence on my fashion designs. The outfit *opposite top right*, for example, is a mixture that I adore – some pieces of it are 18th century, but the line is somewhat 1930s. The picture *above*, though taken in the 1920s, shows my aunts in genuine 18th- and 19th-century costumes. The children *right* are wearing an 'old-lady' style from the Louis-Philippe period, which was popular with young girls in the 1920s. These are my father's cousins, photographed in the 1930s.

The imaginary landscape *above* includes all the famous Arles monuments – I'm proud to have my boutique next door to the two columns on the right.

Madame Calmen *(opposite)* is a friend of my grandmother. Born in 1874,
she is the only living person to have known Van Gogh. She is shown
here wearing one of my jackets.

Above Vincent van Gogh, *La Berceuse* (Madame Roulin), 1889.

CHRISTIAN
LACROIX
Paris

The Nord Pinus in Arles is the bullfighters' hotel. The great bullfighter Dominguin is shown *far left* on the hotel balcony, being acclaimed by the crowd, and he is seen again *near left* with Jean Cocteau. Visiting this hotel as a child, with my father, I saw Picasso and Cocteau at après-corrida cocktails. Now I have my boutique here. *Above* and *below* are two pictures from the family album – my grandfather, and a family group relaxing at a shooting lodge in the 1950s.

Antoine Raspal (1738–1811),
The Dressmaker in Arles.

BEFORE PARIS

n 1969, after the *baccalauréat*, I decided to go and live in Montpellier – the height of exoticism for a teenager who had hardly set foot outside Arles before. I wanted to study French literature at the university and to 'shake things up a bit', in however minor a way. At the same time I was absolutely determined to seek out again someone who was close to my heart. Her name was Laure, and I now realize that she was the earliest object of my passion for beauty, through whom I first became aware of my own aesthetic tastes and impulses. She had a physique that was astonishing and a taste in clothes that was highly individual and most unusual: when in 1965 she used to come to the boys' *lycée* for Greek lessons – quite an event for the school as a whole – she would arrive wearing long red felt gaiters with black buttons with a chartreuse velvet coat over the top. I am convinced now that this is the way things happen in life: at certain crucial points we stumble upon people, objects or atmospheres which prove to be recognition signals, indicating the things that are destined to be important to us, the sort of people we are going to be.

We made for ourselves a daily life composed of imagined idylls and secret pacts, of things that we could not express and others that we took delight in mocking. It was all extremely theatrical and flamboyant: we would play the piano together and act out little scenes and charades, never taking the characters seriously, needless to say. For me it was a wonderful time, a sort of apprenticeship in the pointless things in life, which lasted until I reached the age of eighteen, when it all just as suddenly and inevitably began to seem immature and utterly superficial.

Laure in red leggings, 1965.

The flamboyant little clique to which I belonged also contained other, more outrageous elements. As well as Laure, it embraced a family of rather advanced aesthetes (heavily influenced, I now suspect, by the de Noailles circle), one of whom had known Cocteau and owned Fauré's piano. To them I owed my introduction to the world of Wilde, Beardsley and other decadents of every order and, indeed, disorder. No amount of weirdness or peculiarity was too much for the acolytes of this secret world; nothing was too bizarre. A certain devilishness in these *enfants terribles* impressed me, in contrast with Laure's angelic quality. It was all typically provincial, though

Marie-Colette, 'Noailles-style' *enfant terrible*, used to receive her friends in bed, 1967.

in one respect it was unusual: in all our wildest excesses we had no standards of comparison, and were therefore constrained by no limits. Never in the years that followed have I felt the need to reassess the ideas I formed during this time.

I did not enjoy much else at Montpellier, with the exception of the cyclopean architecture of the Institut d'Art, the firm friendships I made there – often foursomes, sometimes threesomes, usually twosomes – and Henri Agel's lectures on the history of cinema, through which I discovered Renoir and all the other great classics. Cinema has a huge impact on most people's lives, and I was and am no exception: I often find myself thinking about my life in terms of a film. The world of literature came as another great and necessary shock. One of the professors of literature introduced me to the works of Julien Gracq, and his *Rivage des Syrtes* became my staple reading matter, constantly to be found beside my bed. It has become inextricably bound up with my memories of this time, colouring a whole period of my life. I also read all of Delteil's works (of which *Choléra* was my favourite), savouring the richness of the language, the extravagant imagery, the elaborately turned phrases and the mannered style, all combined with a tremendous ruggedness which saved it from seeming affected or overblown. Later on, curious as it may seem, I was to attempt to apply to the art of fashion design the same principle of creating combinations that were at once rich and carefully balanced.

he summer of 1969 was devoted exclusively to the pursuit of pleasure. It was the summer of Jean Bouquin, the fashion designer from Saint Tropez, and of crazy, wild ideas in clothes. It was also a time which can now be seen as the swansong of that element of elitism which always used to be associated with elegance, the world of fashionable clothes and a sense of style. Nowadays, with the growth of the mass media and popular demand, the fast-moving nature of the ready-to-wear business and the almost instant availability of copies of copies, virtually anybody can aspire to current tastes, experiment with new fads and wear the latest colours. Every new idea is immediately picked up and adapted, losing its freshness and becoming dull and mediocre in the process.

Myself at Montpellier in 'ciré' Renoma raincoat – my uniform in 1969.

It was all very different in those days: then there was still something rather provocative and slightly sinful about the quest for elegance, the desire to be at the height of fashion. The world of dandyism had not yet been left very far behind. Unless you happened to be in Paris, being fashionable was taken to mean that you were a member of a select coterie, and that you were deliberately trying to create an effect. There were names and addresses which have since faded into insignificance or oblivion but which then were required knowledge; you had to know the right labels, the right things to buy, the right codes and signals. The names to go for were Western House and Renoma, with a sprinkling of others from further afield, especially from India and Afghanistan. Ethnic designs mingled quite naturally with the rest, and fashion became like a treasure chest, an extravagant pot-pourri of different combinations and juxtapositions, of mixtures of styles and proportions in apparently infinite variety. We took a reckless delight in flouting all the rules, in improvising an art that came perilously close to fancy dress and yet always somehow managed to avoid it. There was a naive theatricality about it all which I simply adored. It was another episode which made an indelible mark on me, one which in any case I never wanted to erase, and which has become a natural reflex in my work: without the impulse to mix different elements together there can be no salvation!

 ust as my recollections of adolescence are clear and neatly 'filed', so my memories of the time that followed remain in spite of everything blurred and confused. I can recall only disconnected fragments, like bits of some imaginary, always unfinished patchwork. Occasionally glimpses of one part or another come back to me, as if suddenly illuminated, but I can never quite work out how they fit together. With hindsight,

Hippy elegance.

however, I can see that this was above all the time when I learned to understand the landscapes of town and country, alone, with no timetable, goal or obligations, with no thoughts of needing to get back or even to eat if I didn't feel like it, wandering anywhere, in any direction, with no itinerary or references, getting lost: in a word, freedom. This was the time when I began to travel, discovering Naples, Genoa, Piraeus, the Peloponnese, tiny Greek villages where they still kept up the traditional custom of killing the sheep: prospects of dust and arid vegetation, sun-filled landscapes through which I tramped in every direction, purposeless and blissfully happy. Images of those days, stored deep in my memory, will always be with me. There was one autumn in Perpignan, for example, with a particular light, particular smells, flowers that were different from the ones I was used to in Arles, the tramontana which blew in a way that was quite different from the mistral, and unbelievable Romanesque churches.

'People of Provence, here is the cup handed down to us by the Catalans', runs the patriotic Provençal hymn, and I have set out many times to test the truth of this sacred sharing of the holy grail, escaping as often as I could beyond the Cathar citadels and the surrealist villages, beyond Collioure-la-Fauve and on to Barcelona. This city still bore some resemblance to the Barcelona of Malraux and Genet, from the Hotel Oriente to the Café de l'Opéra, passing by way of the seedy bars of the Barrio Chino, wreathed in the smells of frying oil and 'Maja' soap. I have always been drawn to towns which ebb away into the sea. I find them profoundly moving: Marseille, my own personal Orient, Lisbon and of course Venice, which used to beckon us every winter.

If this was an era which saw itself by turns as Viscontiesque, Felliniesque or Pasoliniesque, our lives too seemed to echo the cinema: *The Damned, Fellini Satyricon, Teorema* and Warhol's *L'Amour*. Girls at the time copied the make-up of Warhol stars Donna Jordan and Jane Forth, with masses of rouge, redrawn eyebrows and glossy lips. Oddly enough, this was the moment when I began to 'rediscover' my roots. There was no hiding the fact: I was hopelessly in love with the little villages of the Camargue. I got to know them intimately, inside out; I drank from their springs, devoured their smells and tastes; imprinted their images on my mind and stole them away with me. I used to set off in search of the ancient civilizations of the Camargue, of gypsy culture, of my own nature: the happy, timeless south of Pagnol and Giono, which sadly has vanished all too quickly.

hus it was that one evening I found myself at La Chouraskaia, which was clearly the forerunner of great nightclubs such as Le Palace which were to spring up from 1975 onwards. It was a sort of enormous hut, boasting a torchère carved by César and otherwise decorated in a style that owed a certain amount to art nouveau, and designed with a self-selecting clientele in mind, all of whom were friends among themselves. Specially imported bootleg Jimi Hendrix and Rolling Stones recordings mingled happily with traditional music, Charles Trenet songs and high opera. The whole affair was a faithful reflection of the character of its founder and host, Jean Lafon, who had started off by building a modest shelter to protect himself and a few friends from the rain, and finished up by making it progressively larger to accommodate the ever-growing numbers of friends who crowded in.

Jean Lafon is a real character, a genuine eccentric. He has always led a double life, equally at home with the sleekest, most sophisticated of international society life or the wild horses of the Camargue. Born into an aristocratic Protestant family from Nîmes, he spent his childhood in Tonkin. On his

Unisex summer and winter fashion at La Chouraskaia, early 1970s.

return to France he bought the famous Granon herd of Camargue horses, and has borne their colours aloft ever since. He and Marie-Laure de Noailles used to share a little *mas*, a traditional cube-shaped Camargue farmhouse, very simple and decorated in Majorelle and neo-Gothic style with great charm. The decorations have not been changed: slightly faded, rather dilapidated, timeless and thoroughly lived in, they are highly personal and reflect a remarkable approach to life, genuinely fascinating without being in any way ostentatious or superficial. It was because he was so anxious not to exclude anybody that he allowed La Chouraskaia to grow, little by little; we used to spend endless nights there, making our way across the Camargue in the early hours. For me it will always be the place that symbolizes all the pleasures of the 1970s, which I have never felt the need either to repudiate or to reassess – for who can ever turn their backs on the fashions, the style, the flavour of the time when they were eighteen years old?

t was in September 1973 that I 'went up' to Paris. I had been given an introduction to Jacques Thuillier of the Institut d'Art, and ended up enrolling to do a master's degree under his supervision, on the subject of dress as depicted in seventeenth-century French painting. . . .
Needless to say, I never finished it. At the same time I was also doing a course at the Ecole du Louvre intended to prepare aspiring curators for the competitive examination they were required to sit in order to qualify; and on top of all that I was thinking about enrolling at the Penninguen school so as not to get out of practice with my drawing or lose my taste for design, neither of which was catered for in the museum course. It was a desire that was to be swiftly sacrificed in the face of a heavy timetable and demanding standards of work, and instead I began to draw just for myself, in notebooks or on scraps of paper, whatever came to hand. I must confess that I was disappointed by the general atmosphere in museum and conservation circles, where, apart from one or two friendships which I managed to make, I never really felt at ease. Nevertheless I stuck to it, or made a good pretence of doing so, for the full three years, before finally failing the examination in 1976.

HOW TO BE A
FASHION DESIGNER

he transition between the south of France and Paris was altogether fairly gruelling, and I found it hard to adjust to this new life, with its unfamiliar rhythm. Prompted both by respect for childhood promises and economic necessity, I shared a flat on rue Saint-Denis with a friend, with all the problems that such arrangements inevitably entail – especially the sudden swings of mood, with wild enthusiasms followed by equally abrupt and no less passionate coolings off. I used to return regularly to Les Baux de Provence, where with the help and advice of the curator of the Arles museums I had started to catalogue the paintings and engravings of Louis Jou. Jou was an artist of Picasso's generation who from his youth – most of which was spent in the library in Barcelona – had always nurtured a fascination for incunabula and illuminated manuscripts. Later on he

established his own system of lettering, and proceeded to devote his life to printing books and lithographs, which he left to pile up in untidy heaps over the years. He had died in 1968, and his widow lived on in a house which had remained unchanged since the twenties, through which there drifted not merely memories but the very spirit and flavour of a particular way of life from between the wars. She had been an artist's model in Montparnasse, and I was as enchanted by her eccentricities as I was by the guests who used to come and go: Provençal storytellers, famous New York photographers or Russian musicians, the sophisticated and the bohemian; they were the link between the past and the present, between Les Alpilles and Paris.

One particularly gloomy November day in 1973, when I was on my way back to Paris after the All Saints' Day holiday, I bumped into a friend who had a regrettable tendency to be sociable: what this really meant was that he lived in a state of perpetual chaos and commotion, surrounded constantly by passing friends or those crowds of acquaintances in which no one ever gets to know anyone else properly. He absolutely insisted that I should go back home with him, swearing solemn oaths that we would be on our own and able to enjoy a quiet chat, that he wasn't expecting a soul and that in any case he didn't feel like being sociable either. We had hardly sat down, naturally, before the doorbell rang. In walked a young woman of his acquaintance, pale-skinned, red-haired and with a beautiful voice, wearing her mother's fur coat over a tee-shirt, black pearls and white shoes. It was Françoise. I think we were each as happy as the other to have met: I was hooked, and so was she. I can remember every moment of the rest of that day in perfect detail: we ate in a Russian restaurant in the rue Mazarine before going on to see Ken Russell's *The Music Lovers*, which had just been released; we simply couldn't tear ourselves apart. We agreed to meet again first thing the next day; this time she was wearing a minidress in rough linen and had drawn her hair back with a hairband, the way girls did at that time. We went

Françoise, the day we met.

to the Braque exhibition at the Orangerie, and in the evening saw Lavelli's production of the Copi play *Les Quatre Jumelles* at Le Palace. Very soon, and at the cost of the promises of my adolescence, we decided to live together.

It was to be a period – lasting about three years – during which we spent an enormous amount of time travelling, which one could do very cheaply then, taking trains and staying in little *pensions*. This was why I failed the curator's examination, and allowed any budding ambitions I might have had in that direction to evaporate – without any great regret on my part, incidentally, as it was clearly not the right course for me.

rançoise worked in advertising, and it was through one of her friends that the whole thing started. One evening I was showing her the sketches that I used to make when for example I had found the staging of a play or opera disappointing and wanted to redesign it according to my own ideas. In among them were a few fashion drawings, and when she saw these she remarked with some surprise that some of them were carbon copies of designs that she had seen at the ready-to-wear collections a week earlier. . . . She suggested that I should go and see Marie Rucki, head of the Berçot school, who in turn advised me that I was wasting my time studying and proposed instead that she should give me introductions to a number of designers of her acquaintance. This was how I came to meet Karl Lagerfeld, Angelo Tarlazzi, Marc Bohan and even Pierre Bergé, all of whom not only agreed to see me but also showed warm interest in my work. It was the great age of ready-to-wear, which then reigned virtually supreme.

Françoise meanwhile had decided that she wanted to change her job. She started to look around for other possibilities and someone suggested that she should go and see a certain Jean-Jacques Picart, head of an extremely high-powered and successful press agency, who also worked with Thierry Mugler and other young creative talents of the time. I have a clear memory of going with her to the meeting, and of seeing her coming out a few minutes later positively beaming and telling me how nice these people were, and how she would like to work with them. Françoise and Jean-Jacques then came to an agreement, and so it was that I gained my first real entrée into the world of fashion, designers and fashion houses. It was difficult to believe it was all true, and all the more so as it was a phenomenon that was still in its infancy, and everyone seemed to be swept along on a wave of euphoria, innovation and improvisation, all of it wild and crazy to a greater or lesser degree. I can still recall one of my first Mugler shows, at the Cirque d'Hiver, with a whole series of tartan dresses and a finale that was out of this world: it felt as if I were discovering real life, or my own at least.

In the spring of 1978 we set off for a week's holiday in New York. Hardly had we got back when Françoise received a call from Jean-Jacques to let her know that he had been asked to take over public relations for Hermès and that there would be a job for me there if I wanted it. It was at Hermès that I learned the ropes and got to know the technical side of the business. After a few months, however, by which time I was working only part time, I felt I had probably got as much as I could out of it, and began to fix my sights on broader horizons. One day when I was at home the telephone rang and I heard a voice offering me a job; I have to confess, bizarre as it may seem, that I accepted without really knowing who it was on the other end of the line! It turned out to be Guy Paulin, whom Françoise had got to know in the interim, and who had decided to call me to ask me to help him with his work. He put me in charge of accessories, and with him I discovered what it was that constituted the avant-garde element in 'futurist-punk': a modernity that was at once soft, subtle and sharp.

At the same time I was looking after the final adjustments to the collections of the Japanese fashion house Jun Ashida, which entailed going to Tokyo twice a year. Paradoxically, it was there that I learned about luxury, and Jean-Jacques suggested that I should show my work to Patou, who were looking for a new designer. As ready-to-wear was then at the height of its success, virtually everybody had taken to dismissing couture as outmoded, ossified

Late 1970s fashion victim.

and altogether *passé*, burdened with costs that were out of all proportion, a highly restricted clientele and rituals that were positively archaic. Not us, however: I was thrilled at the prospect of such a challenge. So it was that in November 1981 I found myself working in the world of couture, without having the slightest notion of the technical restrictions by which it was bounded or the customs and practices by which it was regulated. I had not the faintest idea, for instance, that every show had to be mounted within a budget. This rather caught me out on my first show, which as a result nearly did not see the light of day; nevertheless, though it turned out to be lacking in balance, it was full of themes and ideas which I am still exploring and developing, and in which I continue to believe.

The idea for the 'pouf', for example, came to me on a journey through Italy, where I was doing little bits of bread-and-butter work, notably shoe collections. I remember clearly how it happened. I was sitting on the terrace of the little hotel in which I usually stayed in Florence, looking out over the Arno and leafing through a magazine of the 1880s. I found myself stopping in my tracks in front of its pictures of gowns with bustles, and thinking that it would be intriguing to imagine 'mini' versions of them on young women of the day. I also felt that fundamentally there was always a place in the world of fashion for the *joie-de-vivre* and imagination they represented, which for me have always been ageless.

From the 1880s to the 1980s.

Looking back, it seems that rather than wanting to create for creation's sake, I have usually tried to modify existing shapes, dimensions and choices and revitalize them according to my own vision; to give them a fresh verve and élan, and to remove from them an element of conformity without rejecting them out of hand. In this way I hope to be able to shed new light on them while still using a familiar source, rather as you might turn a complex garment inside out in order to understand the idea behind it and the way it has been put together, but without actually resorting to taking it apart.

y second collection for Patou was more under control, as I had by then managed to grasp the requirements involved, the numbers of changes and garments needed, and the importance of establishing the right rhythm. My associate and I had arranged to meet in a café in order to face the reviews. They were so complimentary that I burst into tears. *Libération* had published a photograph of Inès de la Fressange on the catwalk and captioned it 'la fée de Patou'. Inès had been involved in the whole enterprise as a friend from the outset, as it was she who had agreed to model in front of the top people at Patou when I had put on a show of work I had done for previous clients. It was to be a watershed in my professional life.

When my third collection was shown, in January 1983, Jean de Mouy, head of Patou, was kind enough to come and find me in the wings and push me forward on to the podium. The fourth collection, on a Russian theme, was a little sad and not such a success, though I am still attached to certain aspects of it. There then followed a series of different themes: the songs of Charles Trenet and the naive drawings of children (January 1984); Bérard, acrobats and Sauguet's fairground entertainers (July 1984), when our first small group of aficionados came into being; my first truly Spanish collection (January 1985), also our first big success, inspired by the dual desire to break away from the rather safe and well-bred 'Deauville' image traditionally associated with Patou, and to explore the myths of my childhood; dance in all its forms and inspirations (July 1985); a collection based not so much on a theme as on a navy blue and white colour scheme (January 1986, my first *Dé d'or*); an American collection, with fur-trappers and Sioux Indians (July 1986); and a Creole collection, from *Paul et Virginie* to Josephine Baker (January 1987).

First Spanish fashion, 1985.

t was during the last of these that negotiations were concluded for the setting up of my own fashion house, which opened in July 1987 with a collection on the theme of Arles and the Camargue, of landscapes and a world that were very personal to me. This was followed by a show on the theme of the Riviera and the Duke of Windsor and Wallis Simpson set (January 1988, my second *Dé d'or*); another evoking the last days of the Roman Empire, Byzantium and a sort of Pompeian south (July 1988); and a collection inspired by Lady Diana Cooper and English high society of the post-war years, acerbic, fluid and relaxed. . .

With the exception of the colour range inspired by Velasquez in the July 1990 collection, I have tended recently to abandon the idea of themes. I seem to be moving – with no turning back, it appears – towards collections which, rather than developing around a story, concentrate on structure, composition, line and fabrics.

When I was at Patou we used to make up virtually the entire plot of a novel for each collection. It was no mere matter of simply coming up with a story-line around which to organize the show, but instead involved elaborating and expanding every possible ramification of the choices we had made: starting with a range of colours and fabrics, the process would continue until we had worked out even where this hypothetical client was supposed to live. Thus for the collection which won me my first *Dé d'or* we imagined that our heroine was a cosmopolitan creature, but one whose voyages took place not in the real world but in her mind, whose interest in other cultures and

Favourite outfit from the collection that brought me my first *Dé d'or*, 1986.

curiosity about other ways of life carried her in spirit to other lands, who had a passion for collecting African artefacts, and so on . . . We constructed an entire world in order to draw from it the conclusions that we needed in order to make a particular choice or select a particular detail, a whole life of the emotions rolled up into a ball and gradually unfurling as the show approached.

In time we were obliged, along with everyone else in the business, to modify and temper this approach, sacrificing some of our wilder imaginings in favour of a new realism. It is not enough simply to produce a good design; you also need to be able to develop it and set it in context, to hammer out your recurring themes and work out your entrances, and to repeat and make variations on a stroke of inspiration so that it enters into people's minds and imaginations . . . In my view there are two possible approaches to staging a show: the 'working session' approach, aimed at commercial interests and articulating an uncomplicated idea as simply as possible; and the 'performance' approach, a showcase in which the clothes serve as a springboard for the imagination, in which the theatrical aspect of the occasion is exploited to the full, and which is aimed essentially (and usually with success) at the media.

Collage by Michel Bonterre, 1986.

large béret

long manteau
housse
flanelle
blanche

Voilà basques
cintrée sur
jupe froncée
courte.

These sketches from the
late 1970s are far and
away my favourites
because with them I
began everything that has
remained in my work
ever since – full, bell
skirt inspired by the
1880s; A-line trapeze coat;
and a gown painted in an
abstract design.

darm
marine

Top These are my earliest fashion drawings – the couples are supposed to personify myself and Françoise wearing our ideal clothes (we weren't too satisfied with the styles being proposed by the fashion world at the time).

I have always liked to work in colourful, rich tweeds. This sketch *(left)* recalls a winter dress often worn by my grandmother.

I think it was the 1978 sketches shown *opposite* which persuaded Karl Lagerfeld to encourage me to be a pattern designer for printed textiles.

en lainage
pour l'hiver

gants
attachés
aux bords
des manches

soie ou synthétique

chaussures en fil électrique
u serpent cuir multicolore
enroulé. En faux serpent
pour l'hiver

paille

The white page, a never-ending sequence of mental acrobatics, kilometres of sketches before you hit upon the right one before you find inspiration, exhilaration. From that point on the problem is not the design but what to leave out. Then comes the miracle of the work-shops, where what used to be merely ink on paper is given life. The dress is

brought down for its final fitting. It's in the fitting room still. Not yet on the "other side", on the catwalk

Ritually, we dress the bride, the last "insect" still in her chrysalis. The others have already displayed themselves performed their part, with all the required accessories. For me as each dress comes back into the wings or ceases to exist.

Their lives are measured by the time it takes to walk down the catwalk and back. I have never witnessed this short step, this

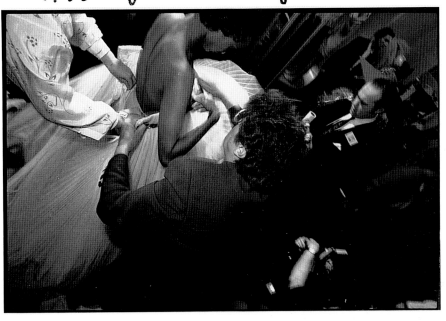

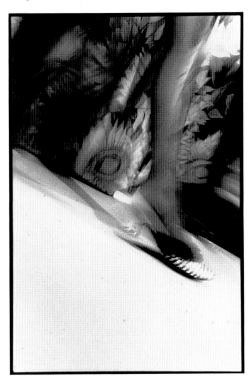

fleeting excursion into the "real world", "live", as it happened.

*

CHRISTIAN
LACROIX
Paris

y idea of England – and I imagine it must be the same for most French people – has distant roots going back to my schooldays. It is gleaned for the most part from photographs that were rather old even then and which served to illustrate a textbook featuring the adventures of the Wilson family. They must have been taken in the 1930s or 1940s, and portrayed a way of life that was utterly foreign in every way, with extraordinary rituals played out to a stately rhythm, and an approach to life that was at once delicate and antiquated. There was also, in about 1960 when I was still at primary school, a teacher who came from London, who always wore an assortment of tweeds – which I have liked ever since – and who sported a peculiarly English haircut, shaved high up into the nape of the neck and with a little quiff left on top. I imagined he must have come from a far-off land where time seemed to have stood still, with something vaguely nineteenth-century about it.

It is never possible to enumerate all the reasons for a particular fascination, but I can at least piece together a few fragments of the puzzle. I have memories of long ago, in black and white, of afternoons spent in front of the television set watching adaptations of Dickens in a series called 'the little theatre for young people', with titles that appeared over a cut-paper curtain.

Agatha Christie heroines.

Looking back on it, the productions were probably crude and naive, but the sets for *David Copperfield* and *The Pickwick Papers*, with their images of a gloomy, slightly medieval city and their evocation of a society peopled by eccentrics or lost children, impressed me greatly and engraved themselves indelibly on my memory.

To this were added frenetic readings of Conan Doyle and Agatha Christie, and later Saki, the only writer who has ever made me literally laugh till I cried; and then there was the world of Hammer horror films, of manor houses, churchyards and forests where monsters lurked or carriages with drawn blinds hurtled through the driving rain. The colours of these images were always in a very particular range of dark browns and greens, with costumes that always looked too new, as if they had just been hired from the theatrical costumier's. I remember too the sensation of discovering Hitchcock's early films, set in England, with their moors and studio cottages, their chases through tiny country villages, the mill in *Young and Innocent*, and Tallulah Bankhead in *Lifeboat*. And in the face of all this there rose the image of contemporary England, tinged with paranoia and rich in humour, as depicted in television series that now enjoy a cult following, such as *The Prisoner* and *The Avengers*.

I would imagine that if anyone were to conduct a massive survey of people of my generation who were brought up in the provinces they would find that their image of England was based on exactly the same foundations, the same fragments of myths and popular images collected in their youth from television, books and the local cinema. In fact, it was only with the arrival of television that these could begin to reach such a wide public.

 made my first journey to London around 1966–67. I was then sixteen or seventeen years old, with my head full of these fairytale images, and I was not disappointed: I had the impression that I was actually entering the world of the films I loved so much. In fact the reality was even better than fiction, for this was an England that was still much more distinctively 'English', more singular and inward-looking, than it is now, more than twenty years on. Women still wore flowery hats, thick stockings and good sturdy shoes that were supposed to be comfortable; the trains still had patterned carpets and wooden surfaces; some of the men still wore bowler hats; and I gazed in wonder at the little suburban villas with their gaily painted front doors in shades of red and green. Soho was still a highly dubious area, and juxtaposed with all this was the extreme modernity of Carnaby Street, where the shop windows were filled with extravagantly bizarre clothes and outrageous displays.

An English family, 1968.

It was at this time that I bought my first copy of British *Vogue* (which I still have): it was the special jubilee edition, and I leafed through its pages so many times that I ended up knowing it by heart. Twiggy was at the zenith of her career, and a Twiggy-like model was pictured on the cover in an evocation of the famous drawing that had appeared on the first edition of the magazine. It was a curious sensation for me when, twenty-five years later, I was asked to contribute to the seventy-fifth anniversary edition: one of those rare moments when you find yourself coming face to face with a milestone in your life, when you suddenly realize how far you have travelled, and in what direction.

The Biba period.

After this initial visit I returned to London only occasionally for brief stays, each of which had its own special character: the Biba era, for instance, when people wore 1930s clothes bought from stalls in Camden Market or the Portobello Road and everything was covered with pseudo art deco graphics. For many years my experience of London remained very much on the surface, which did not worry me in the least: I was perfectly happy simply to wander the streets, every now and then finding myself slap-bang in front of a lighted room, the other side of a bay window, with those tiny spaces, sofas and electric lights, and sometimes, in certain houses in Kensington, a glimpse of an eighteenth-century painting. And I am equally fascinated by the mixture of architecture, with neo-classical colonnades jostling with garish neon signs, which keeps you always aware of the layers of history, each piled on top of the last and all of them clearly visible, in stark contrast with France, where successive waves of change and revolution have each made it their business to sweep away the evidence of the past.

In my view nothing in London is really ugly; everything has its own interest, whether anecdotal or aesthetic. I am well aware that certain French purists would not agree with me in this respect, and that for them nothing can surpass the ordered, monumental architecture of Paris; and also that I risk incurring the displeasure of some English people, who dislike seeing their capital disappearing, and for whom in any case the true pleasures of life are to be found in France or Italy. But I cannot alter either my feelings for or my belief in the qualities of this remarkable urban landscape, at once cosy and faded, the like of which is not to be found in any other country.

espite the fact that I liked so many things about England, it was a long time before I managed to make any English friends. Once again, however, this proved an opportunity to discover a society that was utterly different from French 'society', so rigidly codified and uniform and with a 'bourgeois establishment' side which I dislike. I feel much more at ease among the English, where the worlds of fashion and the aristocracy mingle more easily, and where the fact of 'belonging' does not automatically entail inflexible attitudes or an unquestioning respect for the status quo. I am sure that some of my English friends will protest that I have allowed myself to be taken in by an illusory view of their world, and that I am blind to its restrictions; but all the same it seems clear to me that nowhere else, either in France or elsewhere in Europe, does there exist this cult of the eccentric and the idiosyncratic. Old copies of *Tatler*, for example, with their implausible parties devoted to dyeing turtle doves blue or dressing dogs up in tartan, are brimming with it.

There is something in people's approach to life – a visit to a 'farmers' daughters' club' springs to mind, for instance, or one to another club in Covent Garden which with its smoke-blackened fireplaces and sunken old armchairs was just like a private house – which is so profoundly original and so full of ironic detachment that it seems to me to exemplify the appropriate distance to be observed in relationships, combining a certain playfulness with a respect for the privacy of the individual. This is also something which has always fascinated me about the artistic and intellectual circles in which Cecil Beaton moved. Beaton deserves a place of honour in my little pantheon of English influences in view of the tremendous impact that *My Fair Lady* had on me, as I have described elsewhere; and it is possible that somewhere deep inside me there still lingers the conviction that the Ascot scene, with its mixture of consummate chic and outrageousness, combined with equal parts of irony and the baroque, of high society and the theatrical world, in fact represents England in microcosm. At the time I was completely obsessed with it: I cut out all the pictures I could find of the film, the actors and the sets, as though hoping literally to absorb this world, even down to its minutest details.

From that point on I had only to tease out the threads, as it were, and one object, character or place would lead me on to another. I became interested in the circles in which Beaton mixed and whose members he photographed: Lady Diana Cooper, Edward James, the Sitwells and the rest, possibly because the one thing they had in common and the force which bound them together was a certain kind of 'style'. For the diplomats, writers, painters, photographers, decorators and others who made up this circle, elegance, in manners as in art, was a way of life. Combining a sense of form, good taste and close familiarity with the latest movements in the avant-garde with an approach to life that contrived to be both studied and relaxed, exacting and informal, it was a milieu that was more open and diverse than the artistic and cultural world in France at the time (with the exception of the de Noailles and Etienne de Beaumont circles). This seems to me to be due in part to the underground role that intellectual and literary coteries play in French cultural life, in contrast to English culture which is more heavily influenced by the unusual in general and by the personal visions of individual writers in particular. I loved the Beaton circle's delight in entertainments and masquerades, their gift for spiriting up whole worlds out of everything and nothing, their talent for improvisation, for constantly throwing things together, their ability to be simultaneously spectacular and lucid, and their mixing of styles.

Someone else who was close to Beaton, though they did not always see eye to eye, was the decorator and designer Oliver Messel, whose world I discovered by way of the beauty of his sister, the Countess of Rosse: I remember every detail of her face from the first time I saw it, in the photographs of Princess Margaret's wedding. Messel shared Beaton's taste for ironic allusion, for juxtaposing the sublime and the makeshift, *objets d'art* and everyday things transformed by their context.

I was struck by the same spirit in the photographer Angus McBean, who always had a slightly ludicrous air and spent his life constructing bizarre settings on remote beaches, in circuses and fairgrounds, or among fake Regency decors. It was a cultivated surrealism, at once naive and sophisticated and constructed quite obviously with scissors and paste, where there reigned a spirit of unbridled licence, barefaced kitsch and an evident delight in doing exactly as he wanted to, mixing styles and periods without a second thought and untroubled by the slightest concern about breaking the rules or offending either common sense or good taste. It was this exultant freedom which at the same time gave his work all its charm, or its style, as Diana Vreeland would have described it. And I feel a much closer affinity with the 'improper' surrealism of McBean than with the more abstract and mathematical surrealism of André Breton, for example. Beaton, Messel, McBean: with their piecemeal approach they constructed impossible contrivances, held sway over all that was strange or unlikely, succeeded in uniting mutually contradictory elements, and managed to draw out the most unexpected, improbable side of things. They invented an ever-changing, constantly moving, unstable culture, and only they knew how to extract from it, not the gratuitous mixture that the French would have produced, but a true coherence.

he great psychedelic movement of the sixties was without doubt the most popular and flamboyant expression of this gift for mixing things, this delight in happy accidents and outlandish alliances. It was also the beginning of a new and more sensual response to fabrics, and of a relaxed and imaginative approach which had not been experienced for many years, if ever before. Besides its urban landscape and the photographers and bizarre characters mentioned above, London has for a long time been for me an inexhaustible mine of old clothes, of textiles of all sorts, of the embroidery and patchwork which were then to be found everywhere, from the King's Road to local jumble sales for which old ladies had turned out their attics. I have the impression now that opportunities for real finds are a good deal scarcer, and that there is a growing trade in fake and imitation 'antiques'; but it is still possible to discover rare pearls among the dross, in the Portobello Road or elsewhere, perhaps heaped on a tatty bit of old lino or laid out on a stall that would be more at home in a fairground than in an antique market. And on the streets there is less of the wild intensity and richness of invention than there used to be, much of it having succumbed to that spuriously 'continental' elegance favoured by yuppies and the Thatcher generation, which in fact represents nothing so much as the impoverishment of designer clothes or the wholesale adoption of the worst clichés of ready-to-wear.

Nonetheless, there will always be those moments to treasure, when you suddenly glimpse a hat sprouting a crazy collection of flowers, a pair of shoes hovering somewhere between fluorescent and sugar pink, curious proportions, ethnic details or a hairstyle in all the colours of the rainbow. While I have derived a great deal of inspiration from the nonchalant elegance of the 'beautiful people' of the period between the wars, such as the Windsors and Lady Diana Cooper, I believe that it is in this wilful, stubborn taste for uncompromising originality, this unruffled eccentricity, as exemplified by the Sitwells and Stephen Tennant, that there are still lessons for us to learn. Here, surely, are to be found principles which could help us to define a new elegance for today, successfully combining the classic and the original, without being too self-conscious, and untroubled by the desire to please at all costs.

The most beautiful complexions
I have ever seen were my grandmother's
and Princess Elizabeth's – perfect English roses!

The Ascot scene is my favourite scene from *My Fair Lady*.
On 6 May 1960 – I was about nine years old – I asked to
leave school early to watch Princess Margaret's wedding on
television. I registered then the extraordinary beauty of the
Countess of Rosse (second row, third from left), her
charming hat, her perfect makeup. It was only later that I
realized that she was Oliver Messel's sister.

England: tradition plus surrealism.
Opposite page
Top Angus McBean, *Pamela Stanley*, 1938.
Centre Design by Oliver Messel.
Bottom Cecil Beaton, *Queen Elizabeth,*
the Queen Mother, 1953.
This page Angus McBean, *Neptune*, 1940, surrounded
by a design by Oliver Messel.

What I look for in London markets are relics of 'High Bohemia', the unconventional world of artists. I love the two opposite faces of England because they are both strongly expressive of the deep soul of the country. And popular traditions, such as the Pearly Kings and Queens, not only inspire the creation of wonderful extravaganzas but are an indication of the richness of the nation.

y childhood was spent in those great, bare, high-ceilinged rooms, dim behind closed shutters and exuding a curious odour of damp mingled with aromatic herbs, which are traditional in the Arles region. Even the great honey-coloured stone mansions of the seventeenth and eighteenth centuries displayed a positively puritan degree of restraint in their decoration, with painted or whitewashed walls, perhaps hung with a framed engraving, and a few serviceable pieces of furniture. But this apparent minimalism sheltered a way of life that had remained virtually unchanged for centuries, an *art de vivre* so perfectly conceived that it moves me to this day.

Perhaps partly as an expression of youthful rebellion, but also in response to a preference which I still share, I was equally strongly attracted to the exact opposite of this type of decor, to eclectic clutters in the manner of Pierre Loti or Sarah Bernhardt, crammed with bric-à-brac and hoarded treasures and imbued with an air of theatricality that was both striking and cultivated. At this point there appeared the book that was to become both my guiding light and an indispensable work of reference for anything to do with decoration:

Sarah Bernhardt's style, as imagined in the late sixties.

Philippe Jullian's *Les Styles*. I had a particular weakness, which has survived intact, for the page headed 'Café Society, a friend of the Duchess of Windsor': 'The walls are hung with a blue-period Picasso, a Degas, a Tchelitchew or a Coromandel, according to means. Anything abstract would look too intellectual. This decor could be transferred, with the aid of a few ornaments, on board a yacht or to the Ritz. The two chief principles are: apparent disorder contained within symmetry; and a degree of originality but strictly in the manner of the Duchess of Windsor, Nicky de Gunsbourg or Fulco de Verdura. . . .' All-pervading irony and caustic humour were the saving of it.

Leaving aside for a moment the opulence and social snobbery associated with these kinds of interiors, it is their eclecticism, their ability to combine different materials and styles and their air of clutter which fascinate me. I am intrigued by their ability to take over a room while at the same time containing a sort of coded history of a family or individual. All these decors are also indissolubly linked in my mind with a range of deep, saturated colours – cobalt blue or Pompeian red, for instance, picked out with white – which were much used then and have since remained familiar to me through the pages of magazines such as *Plaisir de France* (indeed, the special quality of these colours, which over the years have come to symbolize the charm of those years, may owe something to heliography and contemporary printing processes).

t the opposite end of the spectrum, representing the bare minimum, I would place the houses of the cowherds of the Camargue: tiny thatched dwellings, sparsely furnished and decorated only with gingham in large red or black checks. I have seen so many of them in the course of my wanderings in the Camargue that I have become intrigued by the idea of a way of life that is both active and tranquil, stripped of all the unnecessary

A *cabane de gardian* in the Camargue.

trappings of 'civilization' and devoid of the frantic needs that we invent for ourselves, and lived according to a formula tested by generations and consecrated by time and custom.

One thing is certain: the complete antithesis of this, the type of interior which irritates me beyond measure and which I could not conceive of ever wanting for myself, is the magnificent period reconstruction, furnished solely with authentic and if possible unique pieces of furniture, all in Louis XV or Louis XVI style or the like, embalmed in its own purism and hovering somewhere between a museum and a stage set. As far as this sort of thing goes, the only style I can respond to is the 'Louis XVII' that was so dear to Emilio Terry. Any style that is transitory, eclectic, out of step, provincial or bastardized appeals to me, be it eighteenth-century Provençal, papier-mâché Napoleon III or anything worn and faded – in stark contrast to 'sanitized' styles like that of the 1930s, whose cool crispness, monumentality and much-vaunted perfection leave me quite indifferent, and appear to me to have more to do with arranging objects than with creating spaces for living.

I have always felt the need for a retreat, a secret lair, a place where I can do nothing very much while accumulating piles and layers of objects, rather like geological strata, storing them up for the day when . . ., or just in case. . . . Nothing here is for show, and there is no attempt at decorum. These are places where I can salt things away and not have to look at them – or at least until sufficient time has elapsed for it not to be too painful. Twenty years is the threshold for me, the time after which the past passes into the realm of History, where one can contemplate things with a greater sense of detachment coupled with simple curiosity, and without being overwhelmed by waves of intolerable nostalgia.

For me a house is thus a refuge (I shall never forget that ovoid, foetal interior conceived by Savin Couëlle – a 1970s Gaudi – on the coast of Sardinia), but one which should be always changing and growing, undergoing a constant process of modification and adaptation, ready to take off in any direction and always receptive to new possibilities, and forever moving in the direction of the undefinable. It should be a combination of the house and gardens of Pompeii with their Giacometti-like furniture; a sixteenth-century cabinet of curiosities; a medieval monk's cell, preferably Cistercian; the main room of a Provençal *mas* like the ones in eighteenth-century nativity scenes; the wood and slate of a Japanese bathroom; an English cottage sitting room with its wallpapers and Staffordshire pottery; a bedroom from an early American house in Connecticut or a Russian *dacha*; the red- or black-lacquered living room of a 1960s art collector; and the workshop of a Facteur Cheval. As for the view, this should combine a 1950s New York balcony garden, a Mimi Pinson garret in Montmartre looking out over the whole of Paris, and a roof terrace above a sheer drop to the Mediterranean.

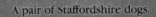

A pair of Staffordshire dogs.

When recently my wife and I had the opportunity to arrange our own personal space, we found we were following the same principles as for fashion design: never being afraid to mix things, however incongruous they may seem, and never resisting the impulse to make collages of different styles. In fact, putting an apartment together is like making a dress, adding a wallpaper frieze instead of an embroidered motif here, or a leopardskin rug in place of a mottled fabric there: basically it is all a matter of patchwork. I did not want it to be too Provençal in feel, because the interior of a building should never be completely at odds with the exterior, and it is impossible to make such fundamental clashes of style work. The sole exception, the one concession to the mythology of the Midi, is a 'bullfighting' dining room in red and gold. In a small Pierre Loti-inspired sitting room kelims and tartans mingle with the 'stars and stripes'. The study, like the kitchen, corresponds to a sort of Platonic ideal. The kitchen, with its stone, terracotta and ceramic colours, could be somewhere in the country and is the very antithesis of high-tech. The study, with its stripes, friezes and 1920s lamps, could have belonged to someone's great-grandfather in the provinces, in the era of Boutet de Monvel and the Marquise de Grand-Air. The bathrooms are very Tartarin de Tarascon, with the *ex-voto* offerings we have arranged in them giving them the air of discreet offertories or private chapels. And finally the bedroom, in pink and pale almond green, with friezes of doves and Prince of Wales feathers, is rather Barbara Cartland. This Parisian apartment is destined to become the natural recipient and expression of all my frustrations and all the things that I feel are missing in my life – a bit of the country, a bit of England and a large dose of folklore; it is my window on the world at the same time as being a reflection of myself, and I am sure that as such it helps me to think and to concentrate.

Although I lack technical knowledge and am utterly helpless when faced with practical problems, I can visualize very clearly the places in which I would like to live, and I also have precise, if wildly disparate, ideas about them. We had just announced the opening of the fashion house, in February 1987, when a magazine asked me to visualize the living room of my dreams. I still have the design I drew up, and it bears a striking resemblance to the place we eventually found to live in: the same range of colours – fuchsia pink, red, yellow and ecru; the same presence of nature (I wanted a tree; we actually have furniture like branches, which reminds me of illustrations in books that I had when I was a child, and natural forms such as coral); the same arches (the apartment that we found on rue Saint-Honoré already had them); the same plaster masks, garden furniture and wrought iron. . . . It was all there: somehow – I have no idea how – we had managed immediately to stumble upon the space of our dreams, simply waiting to be stamped with signs of our own presence.

The artists behind this magical crystallization of ideas were Elizabeth Garrouste and Mattia Bonetti, whose early furniture, followed by their

---

designs for Le Privilège – the restaurant of the Paris discotheque Le Palace – I had discovered with enormous delight a few years earlier. They were the instigators of a process of change that was tremendously exciting and dynamic. We discovered a mutual passion for the same simple, fragile materials, the same precious details, the same ranges of colours and textures, the same space, the same touches of incongruousness and irony, along with a mutual distaste for the rigid forms of a stale and insipid modernism. The result was a space redolent of the worlds of fashion and of theatre, full of its own secret and sumptuous liturgy.

Popular early fifties interior.

n decoration as in other fields, we found ourselves part of a group of friends – painters, writers and informed amateurs – with a shared taste for apparently insignificant or eccentric objects which have since become the focus of a great deal of attention. It is impossible ever to know whether one is the prisoner of one's generation, whether one is reflecting the limited tastes of a particular clique or age group, or whether on the contrary one is part of a more general movement of 'society' at large.

It nevertheless seems clear to me that over the last twenty years we have drifted away from an impassioned discovery of the riches of the world of fashion and towards a fascination for everything to do with the house; that we have abandoned the exterior in favour of the interior, public spaces in favour of private spaces, clubs in favour of private houses where friends can get together in a more personal atmosphere. We are seeing the beginning of a new era, which is not without its repercussions on the very nature of fashion: gone are the ephemeral solutions, the frivolous strokes of inspiration, the brilliant ideas set to last only a season; gone is the 'egotistical' designer who imagines he or she can decree the shape of the moment. Now we are all more concerned with quality and lifestyle, seeking – for our homes as much as our clothes – a solidity and authenticity which we feel represent something of ourselves. And this need not imply a rigidity of any kind; I believe rather that we are returning to a sort of quiet elegance, to the 'bohemianism' of Bloomsbury and Charleston, strange, singular and full of history; to a concern for an *art de vivre* embracing every aspect of ordinary life and the 'ambience' in which we live, from details of clothing to the harmonious balance of furniture and colours in a room.

If I have been strongly influenced by the languid elegance of a certain type of Englishness, by this stubborn taste for quirkiness and this unruffled eccentricity, it is because it embraces certain principles which are helpful in defining an elegance for today, a happy marriage of the classic and the unconventional, not over-concerned with self-examination and untroubled by worries about needing to be acceptable at any price.

In the late sixties and early seventies
we looked back with great fondness to the 'tackiness' of the fifties.
This is a sketch I did then to suggest a kind of mood –
almost Californian.

Ils vivaient tous ensemble dans une maison d'ours, dans la forêt.

When I was a child, Goldilocks and the Three Bears was the story I liked best, especially the version with these illustrations. I'm sure that I stored away the memory of this fancy furniture made from branches because when I created furniture for the couture salon it had similar features. Even my own home reflects the same mixture of patterns, motifs and heart shapes.

Our bathroom *(opposite)* is a patchwork of everything,
including 'Picassiette' made from broken pottery and tiles.
These, and the rugs, carpets and textiles, were mainly
bought at Bermondsey Market in London.

The decoration of the South Italian reliquary *above* contains
real bones and teeth.

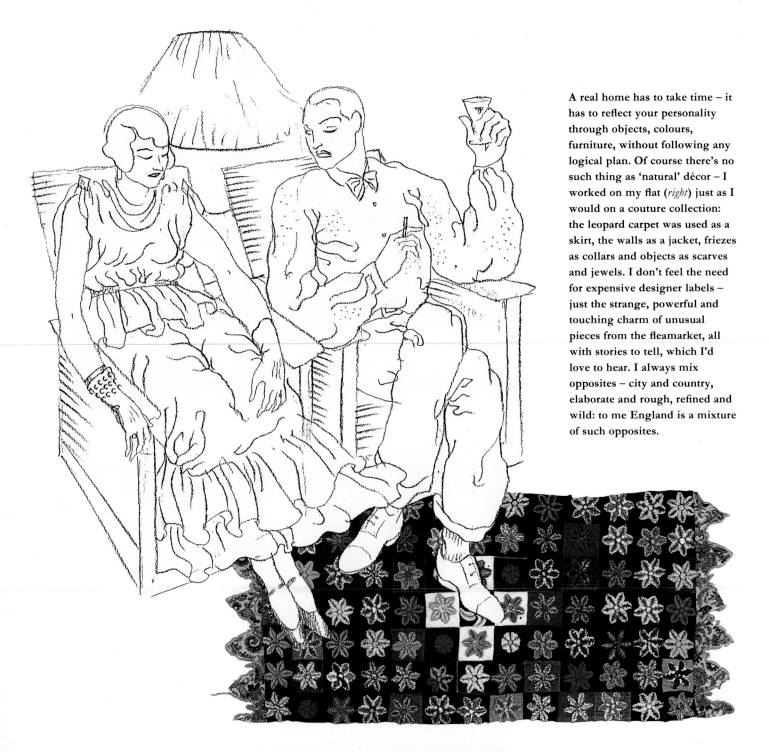

A real home has to take time – it has to reflect your personality through objects, colours, furniture, without following any logical plan. Of course there's no such thing as 'natural' décor – I worked on my flat (*right*) just as I would on a couture collection: the leopard carpet was used as a skirt, the walls as a jacket, friezes as collars and objects as scarves and jewels. I don't feel the need for expensive designer labels – just the strange, powerful and touching charm of unusual pieces from the fleamarket, all with stories to tell, which I'd love to hear. I always mix opposites – city and country, elaborate and rough, refined and wild: to me England is a mixture of such opposites.

Left Sitting room at Charleston, Sussex, lived in and decorated by members of the Bloomsbury Group.

Our dining room, the one room in the flat dedicated to the art
of bullfighting. In the alcove you can see my only collection, of
'Santi Belli' – beautiful, colourful terracotta statues of saints,
made during the 19th century for use in personal shrines in
private houses.

Edwin Smith, *Mrs Tyler's Council Flat, Poplar, London*, 1961.

Above Kitsch houses and the immensely creative décor of ordinary people have always fascinated me. They still inspire me because of their freshness and lack of prejudice or preconceived ideas. Deeply charming, they confirm that there is no such thing as good or bad taste.

Right This is a typical 'cabane de gardian' (horseback bullkeeper's cottage), found only in the Camargue and so different from the *mas* of Provence, only a few kilometres away. As a child I loved the roughness of the thatched roof, the simple furniture and above all the feeling of being close to nature, since this kind of cabin is lost among the watery wastes of the Camargue.

Opposite Edwin Smith, *The King's Bedroom, Knole, Kent*, 1960.

Inset Pierre Loti in his Turkish salon.

I have always liked primitive painters, and painters like Giotto or Carpaccio, because I could lose myself in all the details, like Alice through the looking glass. Here each piece of furniture is so modern, each object so significant and the overall effect so peaceful, serene and strange, that as a student it was my ideal room.

When I was an adolescent I used to work in the library of this mansion in Les-Baux-de-Provence *(below)*. Nothing seemed to have changed since the 15th century – it was not so distant from Carpaccio's world.

Vittore Carpaccio, *The Vision of St Augustine,* c.1567.

In the late 1950s I was the same age as the little hero of *Mon Oncle* and looked very much like him in dress and appearance. Such caricature interiors *(left)* were part of real life at that time.

In Japan the relationship between nature and architecture is highly sophisticated. In my ideal house the bathroom would be Japanese because in Japan each ordinary object is a work of art – no distinction is made between art and craftsmanship.

The mixture of wood, earth and stone shown *below left* is the same sensual combination that I love in the Camargue. The Camargue and Japan are strangely similar – very Zen, very timeless.

The egg-shaped foetal space *(above)* also shows a perfect connection between building and landscape. Such buildings preserve and integrate nature.

Left Early 18th-century Japanese farmhouse.
Above and top right Villa by Jacques and Savin Coüelle, Sardinia.

I found this pipe-smoking
coffee-drinker in Saint Tropez.
Some orientalist 'Santi Belli' can
be found among sacred objects.
The fantasy and candour of these
costumes evoke for me Mozart's
Seraglio or *Cosi fan tutte*.

Theatre and Opera

The fairground entertainments of my early childhood were the first theatre I ever saw. Although these fairground troupes have long since disappeared, the memory of them is still with me, and they have come to represent for me the very essence of the world of theatre, which I always try to rediscover in one form or another in stage productions or in the worlds of creators of theatre.

There was of course something rather sweetly pathetic about those early amateurish performances: the rickety stage, the crudely painted backdrops, the people who wandered around behind the barriers as if believing themselves invisible, the perfunctory make-up, the over-dramatic gestures, the doors that never sounded right when they shut, the clumsy lighting. For the Trinquetaille fête every September a family troupe would come and set themselves up in a square behind our house, their little theatre jostling with the fairground stalls and other sideshows. Two details of their show made a particularly vivid and lasting impression on me: the first was one of those half-and-half characters who were popular in those days, dressed half as a man and half as a woman, half in a dinner jacket and half in a frock, and who played all the roles single-handed; the second was a strange sort of lighting that was both extremely harsh and very warm at the same time, somewhere between Daumier and Toulouse-Lautrec.

In winter there were the provincial tours, to which we never went; but I used to be taken to children's shows (of which I have a memory, picked at random, of a set of a garden filled with gigantic flowers and pumpkins, at which I gazed in utter stupefaction). These used to take place at the theatre in Arles in a little room done up in 1930s style, hung with salmon pink velvet and studded with plaster masks, laughing or crying and themselves covered with velvet: the inspiration perhaps for the masks which today decorate my fashion salons. I also remember being fascinated by the thick layer of ochre-pink make-up with which the actors seemed to feel obliged to coat their faces and legs, and which on occasion – and particularly during worthy renditions of classical pieces – became more or less the only thing capable of holding my attention. . . .

I have memories too of the performances that used to be given in summer in the Roman theatre: of sudden voices and snatches of music that drifted beyond the walls, and of the strange effect of these sounds disappearing into the night air; of the actors' dressing rooms, apparently suspended among the cypresses; of the most eagerly awaited performances of different Mireilles and Marguerites. For my family as for many others in the Midi, music, and especially singing, were part of the fabric of daily life, to be celebrated in rituals that were endowed with an almost sacred solemnity. My grandfather, for example, knew the entire grand opera repertoire and would make us listen to the radio every Sunday lunchtime in religious silence. He belonged to the 'Italian' school of music lovers, singing along with the tenor arias and shouting and booing whenever he was less than satisfied. It was the time of the great Callas versus Tebaldi controversy: he was a devout supporter of Tebaldi, while I from a very early age was fascinated by Callas's sudden swoops from the lowest notes to the highest, and by her sublime passion.

We were neither Wagnerians nor – with the exception of Benjamin Britten – modernists; nor did I care for French opera of the Massenet type, which has now come so much into favour; we steeped ourselves exclusively in the glories of Italian opera, in the productions staged at Orange, and in Mozart as performed at Aix-en-Provence – to such an extent that to this day I cannot listen to Mozart without instantly being transported to the courtyard of the Archbishop's Palace and the productions of the time, particularly the sets, at once austere and baroque, of a Cassandre-like designer. This kaleidoscope would not be complete without mentioning the effect that Rouleau's *Carmen* had on me. It was only later that I understood the reason for my fascination: the sets and costumes had been designed by Lila de Nobili.

bove all, the theatre was something that I used to put on for myself: as a child I would amuse myself by fitting costumes on little cardboard cut-out figures; later I got into the habit of redesigning the costumes whenever I came home from the theatre, altering the colour balances, compositions and so forth. It was all a way of regaining access to an invented, transformed world, where the possibilities were endless and everything was open to change.

I have lost touch with new developments in the theatre since the period when I went most often and most regularly – between 1970 and 1975 – and perhaps things have not changed much between then and now, but that period was one in which there was a positive explosion of theatrical talent and ideas, with an enthusiastic and unqualified delight in every aspect of performance and artifice. It was the time of Chéreau's *La Dispute*, with its restrained lyricism, its menacing use of *chiaroscuro* and the architectural beauty of its set, designed by Peduzzi; and of Strehler's production of *Les Noces* at the Paris Opera. And, along with many others, I was greatly moved on another level by the early *Cirque Imaginaire* shows, which brought back to me, intensified, the atmosphere of the old travelling theatre, with all the playful improvisation of the circus, its mocking tone and its taste for excess. All forms of theatre received a great deal of encouragement of course from the Festival d'Automne in Paris, then in its early years. Bringing together theatre groups and performances of every possible description, it provided an opportunity to get to know their work for the first time.

I had seen on television (there was that marvellous programme about new theatre productions every Sunday afternoon) extracts from a satirical show called *L'Histoire du Théâtre*, performed by absurdly over-made-up actors who delivered their lines in a way that was both melodious and calculatedly off-key, with great play on winks, nudges and innuendo. The whole performance was presented in a deliberately and shamelessly artificial manner, exploiting the full repertoire of trickery and illusion with a zest that was irresistibly infectious. It must have been one of the first shows ever put on by TSE, the theatre group run by Argentinian exiles, who very shortly after my arrival in Paris also staged a dazzling parody of traditional music hall called *Luxe*, orchestrated by an unbelievable mistress of ceremonies with an Argentinian accent. It was so fantastic that I went back every single night. I also went to every performance of another show in a very similar vein: *Les Quatre Jumelles* by the Copi troupe, part of the same Argentinian group as TSE, put on in the basement of Le Palace before it was converted. The actors, their faces daubed with white make-up, displayed the same mixture of violence and detachment, hysteria and irony, plays on manners and witty improvisation that I adored in TSE's work, presented against similarly cleverly contrived and seemingly impossible sets. I have vivid memories too of another outrageous show by Copi which he staged in Montparnasse: I think it was called *Loretta Strong*, and it was a sort of monologue in which the presence of a ghostly Mr Morton was invoked amid a welter of fainting fits and convulsions. Rarely over the intervening years have I experienced with such intensity the enthusiasm, the sense of freedom and the rather childish delight that such unrestrained and wholly theatrical improvisation can produce. But my favourite TSE show, apart from *Luxe*, is not their best-remembered one. Entitled *24 heures*, it took place, if I remember rightly, at Chaillot. Every hour during the day saw the evocation of a different theatrical genre, from the 'whodunnit' to the romantic tearjerker. I would have loved to design the costumes for it.

t was in 1984–85, when I was still with Patou, that I designed my first costumes for the theatre: the theatre company of Nantes sought me out after having seen photographs of my early collections and asked me if I would design the costumes for a production of Rostand's *Chantecler*. I agreed without a moment's hesitation. What excited me most about the project was that, instead of the usual rather routine animal disguises, I was asked to design costumes capable of being interpreted in two different ways. Just before they made their entrances, the characters appeared as sort of shadow-puppets, each suggesting a particular animal: the guinea fowl would subsequently reveal herself as a turn-of-the-century socialite, Chantecler would become a top-hatted hidalgo, the hen pheasant would appear as a well-off woman in a riding habit, and so forth. I found the tension thus created – between the graphic nature of the first appearance of each character and the need thereafter to develop proper working costumes – enormously stimulating.

What I enjoy about theatre work is the very quality which sets it in opposition to the closed, 'egocentric' world of couture: it is all about bringing to life and giving material form to someone else's imaginary world, putting yourself at the disposal of a small group and a production concept, trying out ideas without knowing whether they will really work. All this became clearer still to me when I was asked to design the costumes for a dance show called *Zoopsie Comédie*. I was tempted once again by the idea of the revue format, and the notion of designing for a sequence of distinct, self-contained numbers. This time I made use of the fascination I have always felt – and still feel – for the Molino in Barcelona: a wooden theatre, repainted every year, where an extraordinary array of drag artists perform cabaret-like routines (in Franco's time one of them, known as Cleopatra, used to move the audience to tears by standing centre-stage and singing a *sardane*, then banned as a revolutionary song). I was not only able to introduce some of these memories into my work for *Zoopsie Comédie*, but I also had time to involve myself completely in the work of the group, taking part in

Sketches for costumes for a projected ballet, *Mouse Art*, 1987.

discussions, attending rehearsals and so on. And it was as a result of watching the dancer who took the part of the minotaur, rehearsing, head down and hands behind his neck, that the idea came to me, for example, of attaching his horns to his elbows, which had the effect of producing a radically new and more economical approach. This sort of dynamic, these effects that emerge from the interaction of particular people and a particular situation, go to make up the quality that is absolutely unique to theatre, and which is the reason why I love theatre work so much.

plusieurs volants
articulés en
corolle autour
des poignets.

Left and opposite Sketches for a gown for Teresa Berganza for the opening of the Opéra de la Bastille, 14 July 1985.

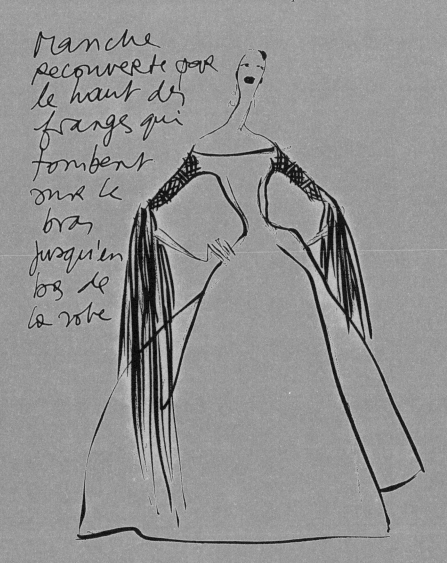

manche
recouverte par
le haut des
franges qui
tombent
sur le
bras
jusqu'en
bas de
la robe

I also designed the costumes for Karol Armitage for *Tarnished Angels*, and for the revue that we wrote with Alfredo Arias for the launch at the Opéra-Comique of the perfume *C'est la vie!* – an evening that was to prove indeed unique, as the revue was performed only on that one occasion. But the two most important productions with which I have so far been associated were *La Gaîté parisienne* for the Metropolitan Opera in 1988 and *Carmen* for the amphitheatre at Nîmes in 1989.

One day Mikhail Baryshnikov telephoned me from New York to tell me that he was planning a revival of *La Gaîté parisienne*, with a reconstruction of Massine's choreography by his son. There was very little time – the whole project took only three months – but I was to have complete freedom to do what I wanted. I decided on a slightly naive interpretation of the world of

Toulouse-Lautrec, based on the idea of the Moulin Rouge and the colourful Paris of the *fin de siècle*, the Lautrec of the posters, as seen through the eyes of Minelli, and in the full Technicolor spectrum, with a liberal use of primary colours, simple shapes and appliqué work. Baryshnikov called me in October, I think; I drew my first sketches and we met to discuss them and clarify our ideas in November; I designed everything on my return and supervised the fittings in December (making the round trip from Paris to New York and back in twenty-four hours); and the show opened in January. I believe it is still in repertory.

As far as *Carmen* was concerned, I wanted to avoid the pitfalls both of the literal-minded, rather amateurish approach and of its opposite, the doctrinaire avant-garde solution. As an overriding factor was the enormous size of the space involved, which left no choice but a kind of popular spectacle, there was no question of simply yielding to the stereotype and I was inclined towards the idea of evoking the period when the opera was written, dressed in the rich and sensual costumes of the Napoleon III era. In the end we produced a mixture of old clothes, reworked and adapted so as to be timeless, and historical costumes: a patchwork of antique Spanish clothes and authentic bullfighters' outfits. In order to arrive at the right range of colours I studied the paintings of Zuloaga and Julio Romero de Torres, with their sombre and slightly oppressive tones.

Given the number of characters and costumes and the distance from which they had to be visible, this production was a splendid opportunity above all to exploit all the possibilities of painting and collage, of mixing antique fabrics and rough canvas, of painting, staining, dyeing and giving a patina to scraps of old clothes and lace; in short, to enjoy to the full one of the principal pleasures – and certainly the most tangible – of designing costumes for the theatre. I should also mention the masochistic thrill that is always unfailingly to be had in meeting the challenge of conjuring up miracles out of a tight budget: the art of artifice in all its glory. A good example of this for me was *l'As-tu Revue?*, an evocation for the Opéra-Comique of a pre World War I theatre troupe confronted by the aesthetic revolution of the 1920s.

These were my first tentative attempts at designing all
the costumes for a play (Molière's *Malade Imaginaire*).
I was ten or eleven at the time.
In the centre is one of my favourite maquettes – for
Karol Armitage in *Tarnished Angels*, at the Paris
Opéra in 1987.

Mouse Art was a project from a young company for which I had designed costumes for *Zoopsie Comédie* in 1986. Though the ballet was never produced, I like these first sketches *(left)*.

Each production begins with instinctive, rough, fast designs full of the impulse of initial inspiration and these often turn out to be the best ideas, on which I base all the others. For *Carmen (this page and opposite bottom)*, we started with photographs from the 1930s.

This costume *(right)* was supposed to be for Carmen in the last act. She is already in mourning for herself, wearing a black dress inspired by the costume of her bullfighter lover, Escamillo.

Opposite top The chemistry between Baryshnikov and myself worked so well that it took us only one week to design the entire production of *La Gaîté parisienne*. The costumes were based on a rather naive vision of Toulouse-Lautrec in a Hollywood setting. *Left to right* The Lady in Green, The Flower Seller, The Ballet Master.

I'd love to design a *Madam Butterfly* production, since it's one of my favourite operas, mixing East and West, timeless Japan and turn-of-the-century Western style. In the 1970s I did actually start to design the whole opera or ballet, just for my own satisfaction *(opposite bottom and this page)*.

Fashions from World War I were the inspiration for this sketch for *l'As-tu Revue?* I have always loved fashions from periods of crisis: in France the largest-scale extravaganzas took place during troubled times – the Revolution, the Great War, the German occupation.

The chorus girls from *l'As-tu Revue? (opposite)* were inspired by the mood of the work of Van Dongen.

A collage to publicize *Carmen*, for which I designed the costumes.
It was performed at the amphitheatre in Nîmes in 1989

rles is a restless town, languid and surreal, where the past rubs shoulders with the present. I love its mixtures and contrasts – sacred and pagan, civilized and primitive, sophisticated and instinctive, reserved and loquacious, classical and baroque, elegant and trivial, light and dark, theatrical and simple, elaborate and austere – and I believe that I am also the product of them. And all this complex alchemy of rich oppositions, this evidence of a history stretching back to antiquity and beyond, is to be found in the corrida and in the love that we bear towards bulls in general.

My first *mise à mort* must have seemed so natural to me that it has not even stuck in my memory, but on the days of the corrida there was always a special quality to the light and the air, an exceptional clarity, fringed with a golden haze and humming with excitement. Everything seemed significant: the cawing of the crows as they circled above the obelisk, the carillons of all the churches, the band playing far-off in their blue and yellow uniforms, the men stiff in their unaccustomed suits, dark still at Easter and lighter at grape-harvest time, and the women in their new outfits. Converging on the amphitheatre from all directions, these processions were quite momentous in feel, and as they wound up the sloping street they took on an even more ceremonial, purposeful air, almost religious in its intensity. As it flowed into the amphitheatre the crowd would become yet denser, and the first Spanish tunes would begin to mingle with the military airs.

The *Arlésiennes*, the napes of their necks shown off by the five ritual pleats of their chantilly lace fichus, their Greek profiles harmoniously balanced by the traditional velvet ribbon, their shoulders thrust back and their trains caught up with a silver clasp, would elbow their way through the crowd to the front seats. In one hand they held lace parasols and in the other beaded or tapestry-work purses, or sometimes the painted and sequinned fans behind which they laughed and gossiped. These gestures and attitudes, unchanged down the centuries, often made me think of Japanese women, so much does each culture seem to have created a traditional dress to suit the physical characteristics of the people. It was as if the *Arlésiennes'* naturally proud bearing was contagious, carried from the tops of the medieval towers to the lowest of the Gallo-Roman terraces, passing by way of the panama hats and bamboo canes of the most traditional aficionados, to be transmitted finally to the bullfighters in the ring below. For in Arles, where the centuries seem to jostle each other for space, the fabric of the town is a patchwork of stones from different eras, a glorious jumble of Renaissance windows made out of friezes plundered from the Roman theatre, Roman portals and Louis XIV balconies.

The *paseo* – the ceremonial march of toreros across the arena – is itself a spectacle of heroic, operatic anachronisms: the mounted heralds, straight out of a Velasquez painting in black velvet and white guipure; Goya's matadors in shrill satins embroidered with gold and silver thread; picadors wearing *Don Quixote* leg armour, riding their horses padded with torn and bloody *petos* that evoke the work of Tapiès; turbulent, frenzied, epic passes, as if from a Gustave Doré engraving; and the mules with flags and bells on their harnesses led by the boys who clean the arena, wearing Pagnolesque red cummerbunds in the ring, and Picasso-like black capes on the terraces.

It was to Picasso that I owed – and still owe – the excitement of my first exhibition, when I was five or six years old. I was completely enraptured by the idea of discovering a goat's head in a bicycle saddle and handlebars, a baboon in a 4CV, Brigitte Bardot in a joyous confusion of eye and mouth, nose and hair, and by the very notion of a game hiding in a work of art. The people of Arles viewed Picasso as one of their own and respected him as such; many years later I learned with enormous pride that cubism was inspired not only by African masks but also by the graphic headdresses traditionally worn by the women of Arles. Cocteau often used to go with Picasso to the corrida, dashing off poems and drawings for the bullfighters, who would then 'dedicate' their bulls to him: a perfect exchange in which neither side ever considered the relative value of what they were offering or receiving.

When the bull suddenly appeared it was like ancient Crete. There would be a dull thud as its horns struck the bright pink and yellow sheet of the cape, sometimes tearing it; then came the feudal charge of the picador, a ballet of *banderillos* trailing spirals of coloured paper, the ritualistic movements of the red cloth, played out to the echoes of a shared passion, and even perhaps of the mysteries of Eleusis and of the great cathedrals. The synchronized rhythms of man and beast would transform savagery into carefully planned choreography, performed in costumes unusually delicate yet extremely masculine; and finally there would be something of a Verdi aria in the elegant display of the pass, drawn out to maximum effect, and the aesthetic frenzy which should transcend the final drama, with beauty becoming to death as humour is to despair: a courtesy.

Cocteau and Picasso at the corrida in Arles, late 1950s.

I have no doubt drawn many lessons, confused but indelible, from this world shimmering with symbols as obvious as they are complex. I would be left gasping for breath as the fight ended and the matadors left the ring: those sombre and fearless maestros, brilliantined idols of the fifties (Ordonez, El Viti, Litri) or smiling and romantic playboys of the sixties (Cordobes, Paquirri). The peons, in costumes embroidered in black, white or silver, would be showered on some days with bouquets, on others with boos and catcalls; the swordbearers would retire from the balustrade of the official stand, their ceremonial capes embroidered with eyelets threaded with gold, sequins or Madonnas at prayer; and the *maletillas* would be bustling about in the outer ring, putting the swords away into studded sheaths and piling the folded capes into embossed leather trunks, sweating under the weight of the earthenware pitchers and silver goblets as they carried them out to the superb Hispano-Suizas. As high as they were wide, and with their roofs piled with trunks and boxes that could have come out of a Zurbaran painting, these sat gleaming and glittering in the sun like great tame beasts, as rich in dreams as a pre-war Rolls Royce.

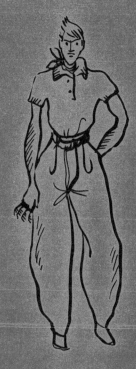

A *razeteur*

nce the fight was over everyone used to spill out into the streets in the direction of the Place du Forum and the Hotel Nord Pinus, the matadors' hotel. Germaine, the *patronne* – half 1930s star acrobat, half American matron in pastel-coloured suit – used to screen her clientele, scrutinizing their bearing and their dress, at the entrance to her premises, which gleamed with copper and polished furniture. Inside, the rituals of polite society took over from the more cosmopolitan manners of the bullfight. The local aristocracy or even royalty, the Spanish supporters with their guttural accents, fashion designers and passing stars would all gather with the black-clad Lucia Bose (who according to custom had not attended the fight), to await the arrival of her husband, the beloved Dominguín, in his white suit stained from the combat, or perhaps in a more daring outfit, green from his *jaquetilla* to his silk stockings.

Afternoons such as these, with their phenomenal levels of wild enthusiasm or passionate disappointment, would provide food for hours, days, seasons and even years of *tertullias*, those commentaries which dissect each corrida in minute detail, assuring the most heroic among them a place in the legends sung by veteran aficionados, the bards of the corrida. It should be understood that we venerate the bulls to the point of worshipping their memory: I remember a cousin of mine who many years afterwards could still recite the weight, pedigree and name of a bull that he had seen fighting somewhere in the depths of Spain in the 1920s.

Another aspect of this cult of the bull, quite different and less well known, is the *course libre* or *course à la cocarde* (rosette), which for many people in the Camargue is the very centre and focus of their existence. The bulls used for this are born in the Rhone delta, and while they share the same black hide as the fighting bull, they are as light and lean as their Spanish cousins are heavy and muscular, with horns pointing upwards in a lyre shape rather than thrusting out horizontally. The *course libre* reaches its climax not in the death of the bull, but in an attempt by a swarm of men clad in white, known as *razeteurs*, to snatch trophies – a red rosette or white tassels tied on with string – from between the bull's horns.

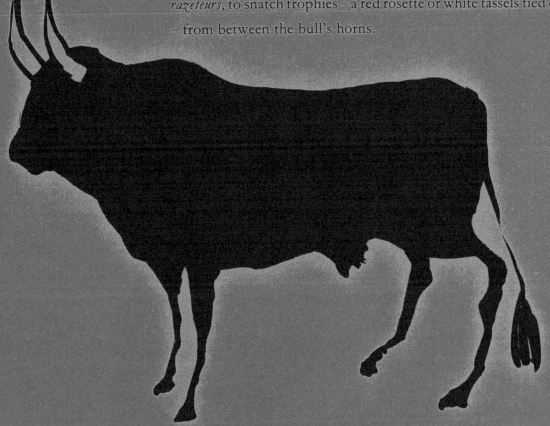

'Sanglier', the most famous bull in the Camargue since the 1930s.

All through the summer months such contests are fought out, in bullrings built out of wood and often planted with plane trees, in even the tiniest of villages. Though they may seem somewhat tedious to the uninitiated, it is on such occasions that the glory and the legend of the bulls, rather than of the men who fight them, is created. The bravest of them, like the historic 'Clairon' and 'Goya', are even immortalized in bronze or stone statues raised in their honour on the squares and crossroads of the Camargue, this land which has shaped me quite as much as has Provence.

f Arles and the northern part of the Rhone represent the refinements of a medieval court of love, richly ornate and draped with exotic fabrics from the Orient; the extravagance of the eighteenth century; and classical ruins in the manner of Hubert-Robert, evoking the era of the Emperor Constantine who made Arles the capital of his empire; the Rhone delta to the south has very different associations. This is a land of mysteries, of intense contrasts almost on the level of Zen Buddhism, an elemental realm where the boundaries between water, earth and sky are blurred, dissolving into shimmering mirages at the meeting point of sand and sea.

A gypsy.

It was the tradition in our family to spend the month of August at Les Saintes-Maries-de-la-Mer. In the marshes there, russet or purple, greenish or lead-coloured, and on the dunes, alight with drifts of wild iris, shells like translucent nuggets of gold and traces of purple-tinted iodine deposited by the waves, it felt to me as if I were going back into the mists of time, to the very dawn of creation. It was on this shore that, according to legend, Marie-Jacobé, Marie-Salomé and Sainte Sara were washed up by the waves, and where they founded the fortified church which as a child I used tirelessly to try to reproduce as a sandcastle. In the flooded crypt, with its suffocating atmosphere of candles and incense, gypsies from all over the world would drape the statue of Sara with layer upon layer of veils, jewelled brocades and diadems. They themselves, with their features from the banks of the Ganges and their black, yellow or orange hair, their caravans from central Europe and their music and dances from Andalusia, would be dressed in a profusion of different fabrics and prints, with wooden sandals in gold or black. I remember too the few streets that lay between the sea and the marshes, either paved or of beaten earth and shaded by cloth or reed blinds; the whitewashed houses with their shutters painted blue or green; the roofs, thatched with straw and topped by a cross; boats with sails in Van Gogh colours; and the glossy velvet and glazed cloth of the Camarguais cowboys, with their battered hats and spotted shirts.

In the little museum at Les Saintes-Maries were displays of stuffed birds with their eggs, camouflaged with patterns that were so abstract, in colours so delicate that they contained virtually no colour, reduced to their essentials like a Japanese wash. They mingled with the black of the bulls and the white of the horses, with just the required note of bizarre surrealism being contributed by portraits of Buffalo Bill and other North American Indian chiefs who had come to visit the celebrated *félibriste*, the Marquis de Baroncelli. Every year we would put a bunch of *saladelle*, the Camargue's mauve-flowered bush, on the Marquis' tomb, at the mouth of the Petit Rhone, where it resembles the Amazon.

Like my father, I used to draw inspiration from these images for many of my drawings-cum-historical frescoes. Very soon this paradise was to fall victim to summer visitors playing at cowboys in houses inspired by a sort of pseudo-Picasso style: early beatniks, makers of abstract jewelry, belated and rootless existentialists – all showed no hesitation in adopting this tranquil corner of the world. Then came Brigitte Bardot, setting the fashion conclusively for gingham, straw hats worn over scarves, tiered Andalusian skirts, and the kicking off of shoes and prejudices. Now the starlets of Cinecittà, and young girls first in Liberty prints and later in pyschedelic dresses, have a definitive place beside the *Arlésiennes*, the nativity figures and the retrospectives of traditional dress that go to make up my personal universe.

A Camargue cowboy.

t is not difficult in the light of today's knowledge to accept as conclusive the results of the sort of research – as frenetic as it was obsessive – that tried to show that, beginning with the late-eighteenth-century return to classicism, each era has retraced the history of costume to an earlier period, which it has used as its inspiration for creating imitations. Thus the Directoire looked back to Ancient Rome, the Romantics to the medieval period, the Pompier school of painters to the Renaissance, the late nineteenth century to the seventeenth century, the Belle Epoque to the eighteenth century, Poiret to the Directoire, and the early 1920s to Romanticism. After a brief interruption in the mid-1920s, when the focus turned to Africa, the cycle resumed as the Surrealists of the 1930s took their inspiration from the nineteenth century; Dior's New Look revived the waspies and sweeping skirts of the turn of the century; Laroche relaunched the flappers of the Charleston era in the 1960s and Saint-Laurent rediscovered the 1930s and 1940s in the 1970s; the nostalgics of the mid-1970s seized on the 1950s and 1960s, leaving the 1980s to rediscover the 1970s; and are we about to see the revival of the 1980s in the 1990s? In any case, and however modestly it may do so, fashion acts as an interpreter of the existential malaise which is the lot of each one of us, attempting in its own way to reduce it to a few fundamental questions. How is it that we can seem to be so constant and yet remain so infatuated with change? How can we set out to experience over and over again the same disturbing associations, with such determination and in the full knowledge of what we are doing? These are the questions that are also posed by the corrida.

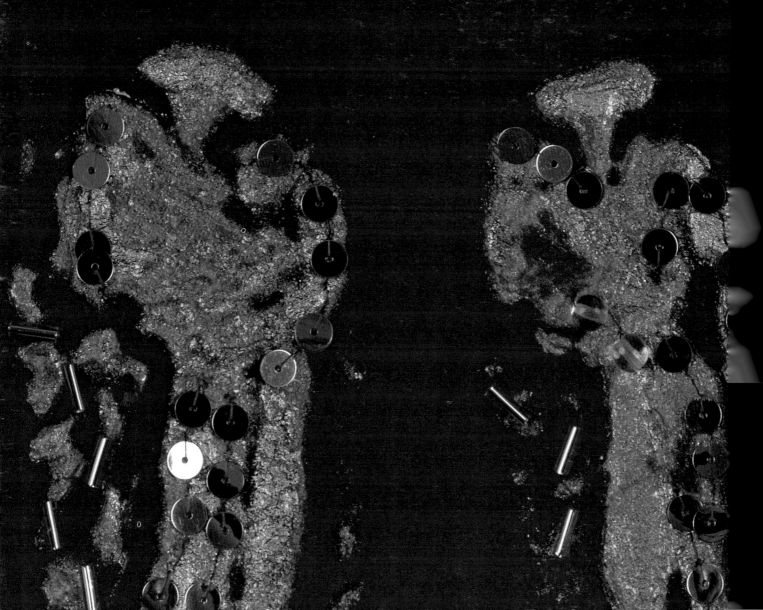

Spain, Arles, bullfighting. I first discovered Spain through
Barcelona and Gaudí. Here *(top)* Gaudí's work and the corrida
are joined in a collage by my dear friend the photographer
Lucien Clergue – he's the thread that links Picasso and Cocteau
to us. In the background is an embroidery taken from a
painting (by another friend whom I admire: Jean-Pierre
Formica), used for a Winter 1991/92 cape.

Bullfighting is as much a social event as a heroic
spectacle. The opening of the bullfight season was
held in Arles at Easter and was something of an
Easter parade – women arrived dressed in
their latest outfits.
Opposite Antonio Borrero, known as 'Chamaco'. He was
19 or 20 when this photograph was taken.
Half-warrior, half-dancer, his costume is a
combination of cuirass and court dress.
Above Photo by Henri Cartier-Bresson, *Harper's
Bazaar*, May 1953.

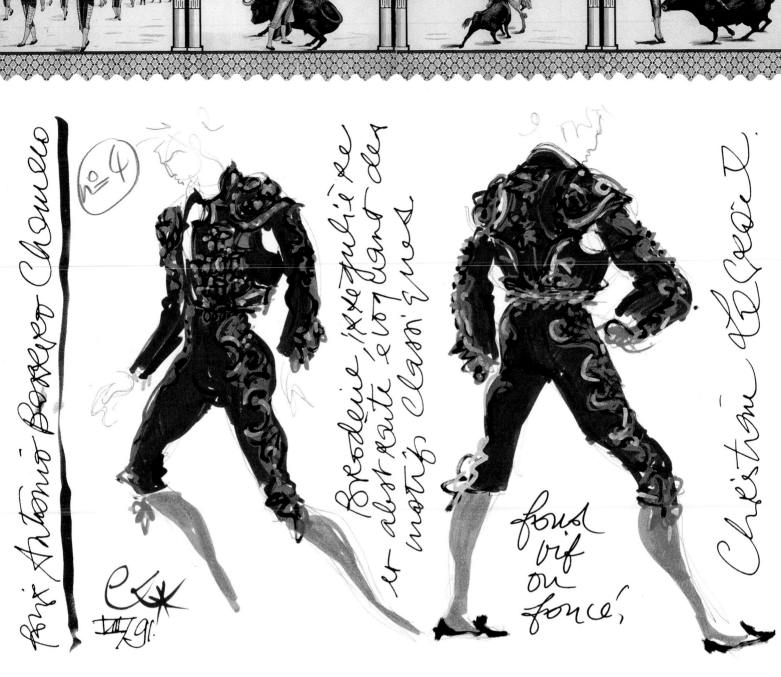

Pour Antonio Borrero Chamaco

Broderie irrégulière et abstraite s'inspirant des motifs classiques.

fond vif ou foncé.

Christian Lacroix

These are designs for costumes for 'Chamaco',
who spent a year studying in England before he decided to
become a bullfighter like his father.

Convent girls once asked to be released early from school
to watch his car go past on the way to the arena.
His name means 'naughty boy'.

The Camargue is arid, black-and-white, whereas Provence is full of colour. *Above* is the cross of the Camargue cowboys, the 'gardians' – I have used this motif often, since my first 1987 couture collection; the heart is for love and charity, the cross for faith and the anchor represents the hope that the daily fish will be successfully caught.

The oufit *opposite top* was inspired by the Camargue and by horseskin and is a homage to Fanfonne Guillerme, a famous woman 'manadier' (bull owner and breeder). *Opposite bottom* The Camargue cross used as a brand.

The Peruvian photographer Martin Chambi,
from Cuzco, photographed this *torera* in the
1920s. I find her look of shy pride very touching.

COUTURE!

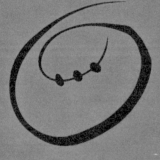

ddly enough, though my livelihood depends on changing tastes, I have never felt any need to disown passing fashions or condemn them as outmoded, or to dismiss once-cherished clothes as 'frightful' or 'unwearable'. I tend not to pigeonhole things, perhaps especially because I have always had an almost morbid fascination for the past – which starts with every passing moment – to the extent that for me everything is imbued with an almost unhealthy degree of nostalgia. I am like the English, who, as a friend of mine used to say, 'have a sense of period'. For me every era has something of interest to offer, if not in its reigning fashions or general trends then in some detail or other, or a way of wearing long-forgotten clothes or of putting together accessories that have long since been consigned to oblivion.

There is only one time for which I have never felt any great warmth, and that is the years 1975 and 1976, when the virtual dictatorship of ready-to-wear ended up, predictably, by producing a sort of levelling down, with the same 'designer clothes' and ready-made outfits available more or less everywhere. That was the point when I felt that on the whole I'd rather go back to the flea markets. The clothes of the years immediately before this (1965–70), on the other hand, have always remained very close, even indispensable, to me, possibly because these were the fashions of my adolescence, when I started to choose my own clothes and build up my wardrobe. But I also believe very strongly that for the past twenty years we have been engaged in attempts to extract and explore different aspects of the fashions of that time, with all their radical innovations.

The seventies – considered as a style – were the age of the discovery of kitsch and all that was 'cheap'. The materials that were used, in the form in which they reached the streets at any rate, speak for themselves: imitation leather, skinny rib-knit sweaters, plastic, vinyl with the transparent film inevitably peeling off, heavy fake-metal buckles and so on, all in aid of a style based pretty closely on that of the 1930s. I absolutely do not believe in the notion of 're-creating' a particular style or look. (Marguerite Carré, one of Dior's principal collaborators in the New Look era, once told me that she had refused to become involved in the reconstruction of one of the styles for a museum because she believed the whole enterprise to be simply impossible, as so many essential though apparently trivial ingredients – textures, body proportions, the model's hands and her imagination, all inextricably linked, had changed: models embody the spirit of the times.)

It was also during the seventies that the element of dandyism disappeared from the world of fashion, along with the overriding desire for originality, the taste for aesthetically pleasing details, for far-fetched names and explosive combinations, and the sheer daring that people needed in order to assert their own tastes and impose their own choices, still very much a feature of the sixties. The work of a designer like Claire McCardell in America in the 1940s, for example, at once elegant and practical, seems to me to be the embodiment of the true spirit of modernity. It also proposes a model from which many lessons remain to be drawn, displaying the same spirit which inspired the distilled furniture designs of Knoll – and which was quite different from the natty trendiness of the sixties in France. Were I to be asked today to name my main pole of attraction, to which I keep returning and in which I never cease to discover fresh complexities, clearly it would be the sixties, just as I was fascinated as a teenager by the Second Empire and the 1940s.

For twenty years of my life the fashions of Paris under the Occupation exercised an almost hypnotic power over me: fragile constructions of feathers and draped jersey, mixtures of sulphur yellow and wine red, a clandestine elegance. And the years following the New Look represent for me in every field the apex of a certain 'Parisian civilization'. You can of course be Parisian without having been born in Paris – sometimes it's even an advantage. Cristobal Balenciaga is the finest example of Italian sensuality and British chic, combined with the natural grandeur of Spain. This cocktail could perhaps only have been created in Paris, and maybe the recipe is now lost. But I hope not.

eople often refer to the 'sixth sense' of fashion designers, to their ability to anticipate new directions in taste and define them before anybody else; and indeed I believe that if anything can justify the esteem in which they are held it is this. But it is not enough to be able to foresee these things: you also have to be able to choose the right moment at which to do so, not too early and not too late. While some designers seem to excel at this game of judging precisely the right moment, knowing exactly how best to match changes in taste with public expectations, I have a tendency to be always slightly out of step, which ultimately has the effect of ruling out certain choices for me.

When I was still at Patou, for instance, I asked the fabric manufacturer Ratti to produce some prints for me in the Pucci style, with those great swirls of vivid colour in dazzling contrasts, on jerseys or other clinging materials. Absolutely the height of 'Italian chic' in the sixties, they were equally absolutely out of fashion twenty years later; and when Pucci did finally come back into vogue, in 1990–91, I was already bored with them and in any case had no further use for them. It was the same, to a lesser degree, with the style of the thirties, with which I used to fill my school notebooks. The whole area is one in which personal judgment and the subtlest of gauges are the only arbiters, where processes that are beyond the reach of intellect are at work, which ultimately we can only observe in ourselves as they take shape. It is in this mysterious process that all the excitement of the business lies; it was also at the moment when I realized that I possessed this gift, quite unconsciously and wholly outside my control, and that it might be able to earn me a living, that I really made my entrance into the world of fashion.

In choosing our moment to launch the fashion house, by contrast – at least to judge by the welcome we received – there can be no doubt that our timing was just right; we seemed to have uncovered a latent desire for a return to the luxury, playfulness and excesses of haute couture. But of course every rose has its thorn, and we soon had to take in hand the heavy, monolithic image we became saddled with, which was both distorted and distorting. Although it gave us an identity, it also imposed its own limitations. Now I see my work as consisting of putting myself in a particular setting and changing it little by little, of directing my clients' tastes towards new possibilities. Gone are the arbitrary, undirected enthusiasms of the early years, the innovations for their own sake, the wild and unrestrained experimentation. I have learned to control certain flights of fancy, when they are in danger of bringing me too close to some fashion or other, and I would like to curb still further the tendency towards a sort of 'fashion culture', even though I am still avid to know every detail of all the press shows and would go to every single one if I could, and read all the reviews and more. But at the same time I must confess that I do rather regret the increasingly dictatorial tone adopted by the fashion press, which is tending to usurp the designer's role in developing and formulating new ideas. In a field where the freedom to create is already limited by pressure from buyers to repeat lines that sold well last season, this merely imposes one more limitation. Happily the fashion house has been set up in such a way that we are not obliged to design with any particular client in mind. I still believe that the most faithful among our clientele will always find something to suit them among the designs of any given collection. Whatever the case, and largely because of the obligations that I have just outlined, it is on the level of couture as opposed to ready-to-wear that my designs have always enjoyed their greatest success.

onstraints always have their positive side, and in any case I always find the creative process tremendously exciting. I love the feeling of having to make something out of nothing, as though approaching virgin territory or a deserted spot in high summer. It is like a breath of fresh air; it gives you new life and fresh blood. For the creative process is like any other function: the cells die off, wear out and are regenerated like any others. Little by little one grows in skill, in practical expertise and in technical sophistication – which is in fact largely a question of nerve.

In becoming a public figure – and in this business one has no other choice – one is inevitably exposed to misunderstanding. People often say, for instance, that the fashions I design are heavily influenced by the eighteenth century. But the truth is that I dislike the fashions of that century, except in some of their provincial and Provençal forms, where affectation and studied prettiness give way to simplified shapes and a certain roughness, or in theatrical versions as worn by the *turqueries*, the French equivalent of the *commedia dell'arte*. I much prefer the styles of the Revolution, the Empire and the Directoire. The side of me that is supposed to be eighteenth-century is actually inspired by the age of the Empress Eugénie, *Madame de . . .* and *Lola Montez*; it comes from some bound volumes of magazines of the Second Empire that I discovered long ago in the attic at home in Arles, which I never tired of leafing through, and which are inseparable in my mind from summer afternoons with grown-ups talking about the war in Algeria, the problems of my grandfather's health and other matters beyond my comprehension.

I have to confess to a certain weakness for all periods of transition, for those times when one order with its own aesthetic has collapsed and another has not yet risen to take its place, when civilization finds itself face to face with barbarism. The Mycenaean civilization in Crete, the fall of the Roman Empire, Byzantium, the Middle Ages, the years just before the Renaissance – symbolized by that painting which has never lost its power of fascination over me, Van Eyck's *Arnolfini Marriage* – these are some of the periods whose

Mickey Mouse was immensely important to my generation. Each morning I woke up hoping that at last I would find him alive, next to me.

shapes and motifs exercise such a strong hold on my imagination. And, at a more domestic level, when as a child I started drawing my own histories of fashion with little painted figures, I very quickly came up against two major stumbling blocks: there always seemed to be a veil of silence drawn over the years immediately before and after both World Wars. These shadowy areas, like small black holes, became all the more intriguing because they were so recent, and because I could not see any reason why they should be made so mysterious. I therefore embarked on an obstinate and determined quest to piece together the styles of those years, scrutinizing Charlie Chaplin films, for instance, or poring over prints from the time. Lartigue's photographs were another mine of ideas. And I cannot begin to describe the effect that *My Fair Lady* had on me, with its costumes by Beaton capturing the essence of Edwardian elegance with their graceful silhouettes and delicate colours, and the superb images of the Ascot scene. All these immediately became fresh focal points for my obsession with the airy elegance, discreet opulence and sheer imaginative extravagance that I had already discovered in the fashions of the Second Empire.

nother set of equally strong influences, though they could not have been more different, derived from aspects of American culture (in this respect I must be fairly typical of a whole post-war generation, born at a time when Europe owed so much to American intervention). Mickey Mouse was the hero of my childhood; he took on a mythical stature to which I am not impervious even now. I religiously collected the Mickey Mouse comic, which came out every Thursday, and I can still remember my amazement when someone gave me some bound volumes of back numbers published before I was born. I could not believe my eyes, as it seemed self-evident to me that Mickey Mouse had been born at the same time as me, and more or less for my benefit; so it was impossible to imagine that he could have existed before I did. It was my first experience of time, the moment when I first became aware of the existence of history. At the same time and running parallel to all this, we had a neighbour with modernist tastes; his house was full of the most 'exotic' prints, fabrics and furniture at which I gazed in wonder, and which it would have been quite impossible to imagine in the traditional interiors that I was used to. And musical comedies were another powerful influence on me right from the start, again like many others of my generation: I must have seen *Banana Split*, starring Carmen Miranda, at least ten times, without its charm ever wearing thin.

For me America consisted of certain kinds of lighting, particularly in my parents' bedroom, which for some inexplicable reason seemed to me to be wholly cinematographic: a *film noir* light diffused by a pink lampshade. It was also encapsulated in the illustrations in the *Petits livres d'or*, the small, golden-spined children's books, and in the Sunday newspapers sent to us occasionally from a small town with which Arles was twinned, and where I also had a penfriend. Looking back, it is impossible to convey the sense of wonder that pervaded my whole being in the presence of these objects which seemed literally to have come from another world, from a land that was more imaginary than real. In the books of my childhood I discovered the exoticism of 'Early America', made up of patchwork quilts, and in the newspapers I found photos of the lacquered 'helmet' hairstyles and trim suits of astronauts' wives.

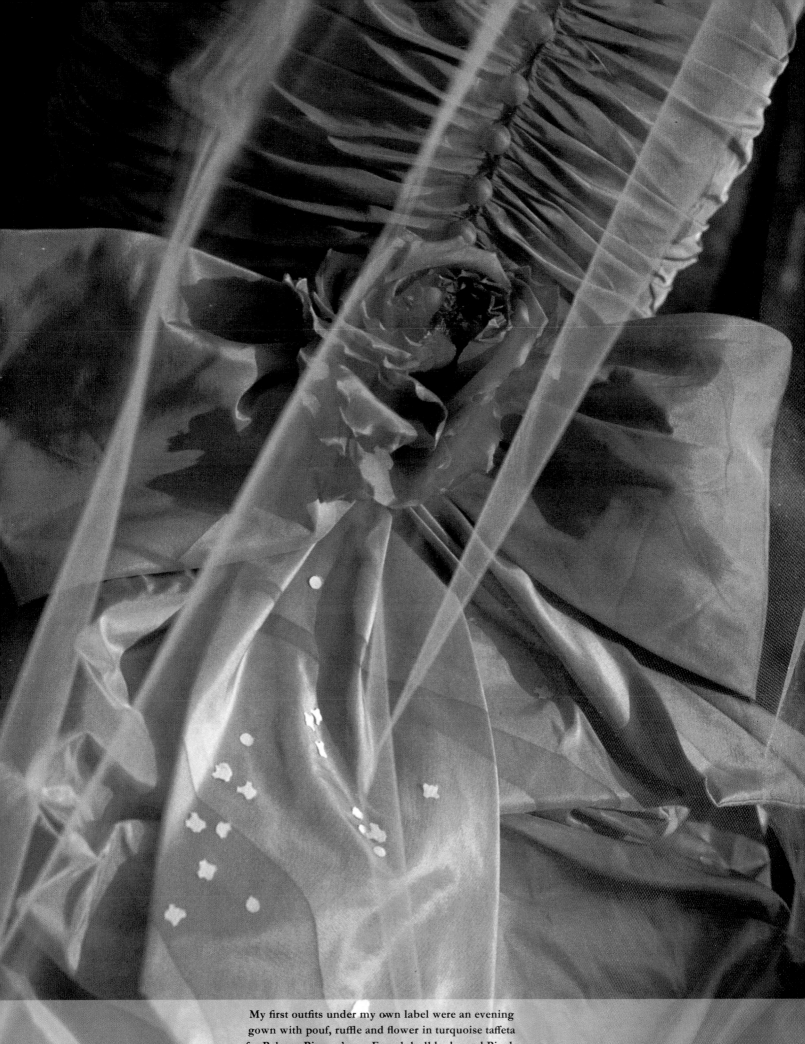

My first outfits under my own label were an evening
gown with pouf, ruffle and flower in turquoise taffeta
for Paloma Picasso's . . . French bulldog! – and Pia de
Brantes' wedding dress – a cloud of salmon pink faille
for the church ceremony which could then be
removed for dinner. Later at night the sleeves were
taken off, leaving a kind of draped swimsuit.

The summery, floral look shown here is very French
to English eyes and very English to the French.

The jacket *right*, made from flowers and lace appliquéd
on to silk, is from the haute couture Summer 1989
collection, which was a homage to Lady Diana
Cooper. The 'bride of the summer' gown *(far right)*,
from the same collection, was inspired by Napoleon
III wallpaper.

Above **Fashion photograph by Cecil Beaton, 1946.**
Top right **Claude Monet,** *Women in the Garden,* 1866–67.

For me hats are the dot on the 'i', the final detail which brings a kind of perfection. The hat adds allure, proportion and mood to the silhouette. Streets lost a lot of charm and wit when the hat disappeared. This is another reason for my love affair with England: as a child I was so impressed by royal hats. I was also charmed by the incredibly wide mountains of ribbons, feathers and flowers from the revolutionary period and from the first decade of the 20th century. And how I love the Mad Hatter!

Top left to bottom right **CL haute couture, S/S 1988; Thomas Gainsborough (1727–88),** *Study of a Lady,* **detail; CL haute couture, A/W 1990/91; Thomas Rowlandson (1756–1827),** *An Old Member on His Way to the House of Commons,* **detail; CL haute couture A/W 1987/88; Victorian engraving; CL haute couture A/W 1991/92; Thomas Rowlandson,** *Box Lobby Loungers,* **detail; CL haute couture, S/S 1988; Thomas Gainsborough,** *Study of a Lady,* **detail.**

One of my favourite museums is San Martino in Naples.
It is full of 18th-century *presepe* – highly naturalistic
figures, all dressed in genuine embroidered clothes.
Below right Jacket, couture collection, Summer 1988.
Left The Macareña Virgin from Seville – the best dressed
Virgin of every year.
Below left Bodice, couture collection, Autumn/Winter
1988/89.
Opposite **Presepe**, San Martino, Naples, photo by Massimo
Listri.

Various cultural influences are apparent in my haute couture collections of Autumn/Winter 1990/91. The jacket at the *left* was inspired by Velasquez and by Spanish wrought iron; the jacket *below left* by gypsy costume; the *torero* jacket *below* by Goya; and the belt *opposite* by 17th-century armour.

Various elements from the fifties and sixties – the witty, cool gestures of fashion models in magazines; the well-bred, unapproachable allure that was admired in movies; the real-life personalities and socialites who also embodied these qualities – still influence my sketches and styles, resulting in eccentric accessories, sunglasses, colours and poses.

Left, top to bottom Tippi Hedren; Anita Ekberg; *Bell, Book and Candle*, 1958; Capucine; *La Dolce Vita*, 1960.

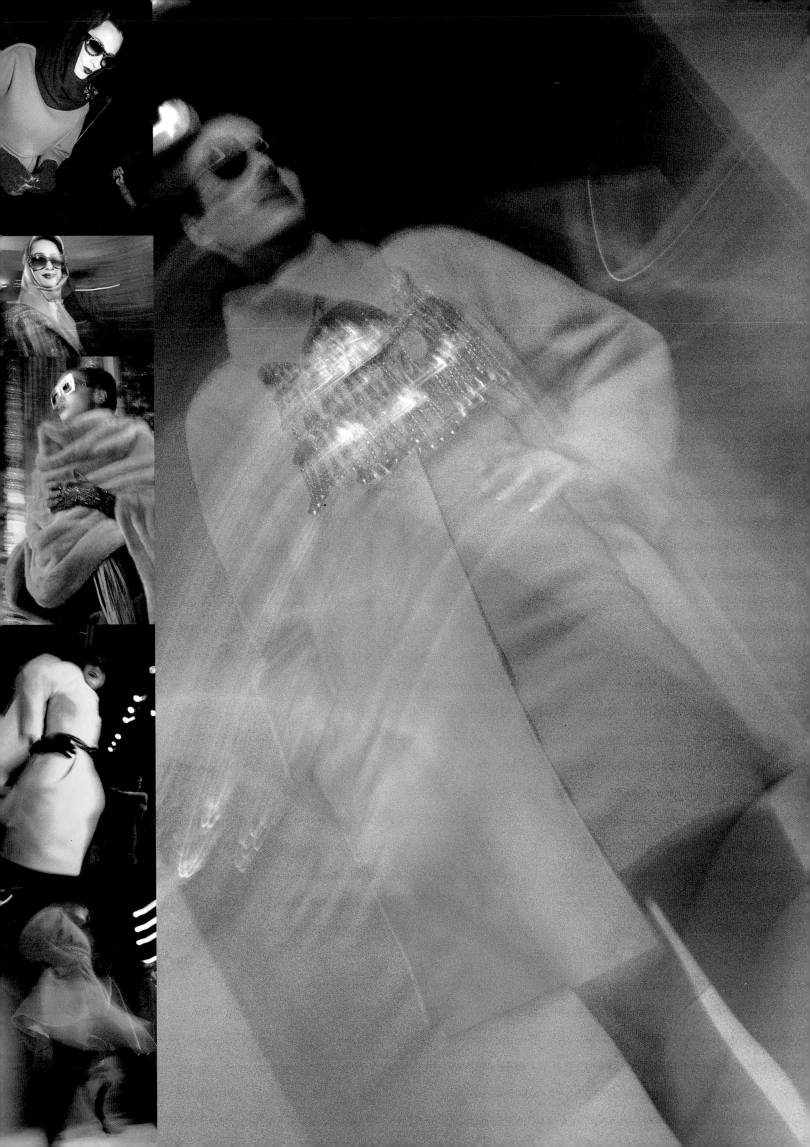

I've always been inspired by both the past and 'elsewhere', because everything rooted in tradition is beautiful, because ethnic clothes and jewels are timeless and, above all, because I believe in a future which mixes cultures, peoples and customs. The real richness comes in the exchanging of these things.

Left to right A 1970s sketch, a genuine 19th-century coat from the Middle East, and a 'Persian' and 'African' coat from the 1990 collections, with a Spanish shawl as background.

Primitivism, roughness, candour
... naive children's paintings ...
abstract paintings like those of
the COBRA group ... the simple
strength of a free brushstroke ...
All these are for me the oxygen
of life, a joy and an inspiration.

I love to run away in my imagination to the world of circus and music-hall – the world of comedy. Nineteenth-century acrobats inspired many of my couture catsuits and even my costumes for ice-skating champions. Small troupes of children, such as those poignantly photographed *opposite far right* in Arles in 1953 by Lucien Clergue, remain in my mind. I was fascinated, too, to discover the English painter Laura Knight for the first time.

Above centre **Laura Knight,** *The Last Act*, 1929.

I always use lace as a lucky charm
and one particular pattern finds its
way into every collection because
lace – black, white or gold – is one
of the most 'couture' of materials.
It belongs also to Spain and
Arlésienne costume and of course
to the turn of the century. Some of
these designs are inspired by an
ecclesiastical costume I found in a
flea market in Madrid; another by
the gown of a Russian princess;
another is cut from an Italian
tablecloth!
Above, top Still from *Mme de . . .* by
Max Ophüls, 1953.
Far right, centre The Irish dancer
Lola Montez, heroine of Max
Ophüls' 1955 film of the same
name.

In these sketches for the Spring/ Summer 1992 couture collection I wanted to capture the atmosphere of a summery *Nutcracker* or a French garden from one of Charles Trenet's songs, as well as the South American mood of Offenbach's *La Périchole* – because, after all, couture doesn't belong to everyday life.

CHRISTIAN LACROIX
Haute-Couture

These sketches are from
the Autumn/Winter
1992/93 ready-to-wear
collection. They embody a
mannish spirit inspired by
the fashions of Madrid,
London and Paris suburbs
in the 1920s and 1930s.

ndoubtedly countless different influences come together in the clothes I design without my even being aware of them, and this is something that is very hard to explain to anyone who is not part of the fashion world. Yet people often ask me how a collection comes into being, what the impulses are from which it springs, the processes by which it takes shape? All I can do in answer to these questions is to sketch out, as far as I am able, the principal stages in the development of a collection. The first question to be answered, at the very outset, is: couture or ready-to-wear? The former will allow more creative freedom and a looser, more 'impressionist', rein on the imagination; the latter needs a more commercial approach, with a shrewder eye on the market.

When that question has been answered, the next step is to picture a woman who embodies the mood of the moment, the new season's theme, and to imagine her in movement; then to set her against a rudimentary scenario, the sketchiest outlines of a story. This imaginary scene-setting is the process which helps one to grasp and distil a kind of mysterious essence, the crystallization of a thousand different clues and signals. These come both from the outside world, in response to the mood of the times, and from my own inner world, reflecting the impulses that awake particular associations, desires or images in me: together they make a strange and heady mixture, at once wholly abstract and enormously sensual, an alchemy which often makes me feel like the sorcerer's apprentice.

Once my theme has emerged and the thread of the story can be traced, the next stage is to reduce it to its component parts, work out different ways of putting them back together again and explore the various possibilities. In the past I used at this point to go to the library to engage in massive operations involving sifting through tons of papers, dusty documents and ancient magazines, as if hoping to find some miracle formula to interpret my dreams. I was invariably disappointed, but in fact I needed to immerse myself in these piles of drawings and photographs in order to forget them again

Sketch for couture collection,
Autumn/Winter 1991/92.

immediately, so that things would start to stir and fall into place in my mind, and work could begin. It is a euphoric feeling, tinged with anxiety, as you veer between a delight in the great wealth of raw material, verging on an *embarras de richesse*, allied to an absolute confidence in your ability to 'get there' in the end, and the ever-present fear of losing your way among it all. And there is also the constant risk of allowing yourself to get sidetracked by gimmicks, by solutions that depend too much on allusion, by straight quotations, by ready-made formulae, and by reinventions of old patterns and shapes which distract you from the creation of a definitive 'look'.

I am less tempted nowadays than I used to be in the early days to seek solutions that I would now describe as rather obvious; I am less likely to turn to ethnic or oriental motifs, for example. I am certainly more open, more receptive, more aware of signs that can present themselves and of chance encounters; more accessible to unexpected ideas that may be triggered by a particular book, film or exhibition, or even a face spotted at the corner of some street. I design much more from scratch, while still keeping the idea of using a different range of tones for each collection: characteristic Provençal shades for the 'boutique' collection; more classic for the mid-season 'cruise' collection, concentrating on a restrained selection of colours and fabrics. (Incidentally, I believe the future lies in 'capsule' collections such as these, based on a limited range of designs in coordinated colours and prints but presented more frequently, and so scattering ideas more liberally: a long way, in short, from the stockpiles of designs presented six months apart at the ready-to-wear shows).

As I have said before, and perhaps in reaction to the way in which people have tended to focus on what is often described as the theatrical, 'decorative' side of my work, I am now much more interested in concentrating on using the cut of a garment alone to define its look and proportions, rather than putting the emphasis on sensational and easily copied details. This might involve, for instance, inventing a new and rather hybrid calf-length look, somewhere between the New Look and the proportions of the eighteenth century; but I would be unable to say at this stage what shape this idea would ultimately take, what sort of journey it will have undergone between the time of writing these words, the time when they are put into print, and the time when my work finally reaches fruition.

All I know is that, while forever following the track of some mysterious Ariadne's thread, I shall always oscillate between a chaste delight in purity of form and a rapturous intoxication with ornamentation. For couture is both these things at the same time. I know that I shall always have a horror of empty space, and that I shall always fill it relentlessly with flowers or paintings – even though I have also experienced the exhilaration to be had in

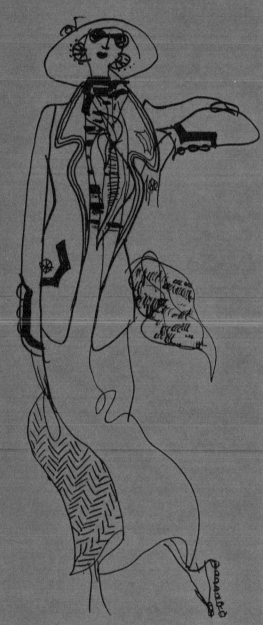

Sketch for couture collection,
Spring/Summer 1992.

black and white. I know that I shall always dot the 'i's of my designs with hats out of Lartigue, taken from a coloured print of ladies skating in the reign of Louis XVI which used to hang beside my bed when I was a child, or from the craziness of a New York Easter Parade, which I discovered with incredulous elation in 1961 or 1962. I know that I shall always be a Mediterranean of the bullring, of the *lices*, and of those processions where style mingles with show, gypsies from the banks of the Ganges with Kensington bohemians. And I know that I shall always enjoy true snobbery, when it signifies a genuine difference – sadly now disappearing in matters of elegance – just as much as the modest sequins of the fairground entertainers.

here are always successive layers of inspiration in creating a collection and I think of myself as an explorer in the world of the imaginary, who believes in combining things that are normally contrasted. A small, Goya-inspired jacket is worn over a tank top, a part of an eighteenth-century costume harmonizes with a sailor's vest. The coat that opened the 1990/91 show was inspired by the oilskins worn by roadgangs in New York, banded with fluorescent strips . . . . You can also discover wrought-iron work from Toledo, the austerity of Castille, the allure of Haile Selassie or the last Kings of Africa. Whether they come from the Camargue, Benin, Sweden or Poland, I adore all those popular crafts and traditions which know spontaneously how to combine the rough with the refined, freshness with frivolity, discipline with improvisation. Such cross-breedings are the bedrock of fashion.

Today I am more rigorous than I used to be, but this does not mean that I have put all my past inspirations aside. Doubting one's loves is still the best way of staying faithful to them. But in my current designs, the primitive simplicity of the Camargue triumphs over Provençal fancy. My Spain of today is now less the Spain of Carmen and more the Spain of Las Meninas and the Moors.

Sketch for couture collection,
Spring/Summer 1990.

I do not deny my roots, but my design research has of late been more Romanesque, more structural. I am now trying to develop even further the basic ingredients of my craft: shape, volume, structure and construction, especially with regard to suits. This focus on the basics has no need of impressions from the past and it tends to tone down colour.

But of course I am addicted to the past to some extent; I'm especially nostalgic about the 1960s – a decade that enjoyed the tail end of an 'art de vivre' of which we have lost the secret. What I especially appreciate in Jacques Demy's movies such as *Les Demoiselles de Rochefort* or in Jean-Paul Rappeneau's *La Vie de château* or Philippe de Broca's *Le Diable par la queue*, among other examples, is their way of being modern, even ahead of their time, without losing a specifically French freshness, culture and spirit. Aping Americans is not the best way of appealing to them. In 1960 Audrey Hepburn could only have been dressed in Paris couture, and it was the imaginativeness of that haute couture that we sought to recreate in the early 1980s. It was a golden legend from which we drew visions of absolute sophistication. The danger is of course that such a look might culminate in a completely humourless 'Sunday best' appearance. A real woman is not like the cover of a magazine. I dread the 'command performance' aspect of couture just as much as I dread conformism.

I am trying to mix basic classics with the more eccentric details – to create a balance between elegance and relaxation – to suit the women of today, who are much freer and less constrained in what they wear. Nowadays a woman can go skiing in pearls or go nightclubbing in a ballgown if she feels like it. The important thing is that she feels comfortable and at ease. The idea that being relaxed means necessarily wearing jeans and a T-shirt is absurd. Some women look more ill-at-ease in jeans than others do in crinolines.

 show is not an end in itself. Why make another collection if everything is planned in advance? It is too often said that we sell dreams. On the contrary, I believe that I start from a very realistic viewpoint by expressing in my shows what many women secretly dream about. I believe in the experimental, exploratory role of couture. And even if there is a certain time lag with my research, I am always anxious to keep a firm grasp on daily life, not in order arbitrarily to parody reality, but in order to sublimate its happier moments.

I refuse to envisage my evolution as a couturier as a series of abrupt changes. I believe that we often have only one thing to say – just as it is said that a great novelist always writes the same book – but that this one thing is constantly evolving. It is this constancy within change which determines a style. One may choose different lengths, for example, from the very short to the very long (paradoxically, I prefer the latter for summer). And there are many different silhouettes. But there is no such thing as a Lacroix uniform. I never design with any particular woman in mind, but for multi-faceted clients who are confident about fashion and can play about with whatever I propose.

My strategy is to have no strategy. For me, couture is like fresh air. I create shapes impulsively, with no preconceived plan. I have worked like this for ten years and have no intention of changing. To begin with, I extolled the virtue of eccentric, barely wearable couture. Then there was a return to legitimacy, to daily life, as if to show that we too could create the classics. Today, what more can I say? Couture will always be couture . . . crazy, contradictory, full of surprises and – above all – stronger than I am.

LIST OF COLLECTIONS

Presentation	Season	Collection	Themes and Features
July 1987	Autumn/Winter 1987/88	Haute Couture	Camargue Provence Bullfighting
October 1987	Spring/Summer 1988	Luxe	Childlike naïveté Flowers Little girls' sketches and dolls
January 1988		Haute Couture	The South of France, from Van Gogh to Wallis Simpson The Mediterranean Naive abstract graphics Picasso
March 1988	Autumn/Winter 1988/89	RTW	Plain colours Simple clothes in bright colours Ethnic prints Ethnic embroideries
		Luxe	Spirit of the forties, with very short skirts
July 1988		Haute Couture	The Byzantine period Pompeii Crèches

Presentation	Season	Collection	Themes and Features
October 1988	Spring/Summer 1989	RTW	Ethnic, Indian mixed with South of France
		Luxe	Tacky, sixties style in the U.S. Barbie doll (with soundtrack from sixties television series)
January 1989		Haute Couture	Lady Diana Cooper and Cecil Beaton
March 1989	Autumn/Winter 1989/90	RTW	Sixties New York, sharp shapes Thirties England, with patchworks and crazy patchworks for knitwear
		Luxe	Breakfast at Tiffany's Embroidered brocade Fur
July 1989		Haute Couture	Patchwork A mix of fabrics
October 1989	Spring/Summer 1990	RTW	Mix of luxury and 'camping'
		Luxe	'Douce France', in Philippe de Broca's and Jean-Paul Rappeneau's sixties movies' style
January 1990		Haute Couture	Circus Musicals Pastel shades

Presentation	Season	Collection	Themes and Features
March 1990	Autumn/Winter 1990/91	RTW	Pioneer/Wild West
		Luxe	Paris/Seville
July 1990		Haute Couture	Velasquez Goya Shades of black
October 1990	Spring/Summer 1991	RTW	Graphic, orientalist and Provençal
January 1991		Haute Couture	Black, white and grey
March 1991	Autumn/Winter 1991/92	RTW	Simple, Hispanic and geometric
July 1991		Haute Couture	Modern gypsies, travellers, nomads Free women
October 1991	Spring/Summer 1992	RTW	'Sun Day' (sunny day and Sunday), with gypsies, sailors and garden parties
January 1992		Haute Couture	'Jardin extraordinaire', from Charles Trenet's song
March 1992	Autumn/Winter 1992/93	RTW	Masculine style with feminine details Contemporary folklore: London street scenes, Andalusian 'campo', China

ACKNOWLEDGMENTS

My gratitude to the staff of Thames and Hudson, in both London and Paris (whose keen enthusiasm Françoise and I have much appreciated), hardly needs to be expressed.

I should also like particularly to thank Sylvain Bergère for giving me five years of fashion show pictures; Lucien Clergue for pictures of Gaudí and Jacques Torregano for one of Chamaco; the Hotel Nord Pinus and the Musée Réattu in Arles for those of Dominguín and Raspal; Marie Martinez, Florence Venturi and Anh Duong for theirs; Fabio Bellotti for his fabrics; Billy-Ron Hadley and the pupils of the Ecole de la rue Paul Valéry, Paris XVIe, for their drawings; finally Lars Nilsson, and many more whom I am sure I must have overlooked.

SOURCES OF ILLUSTRATIONS

Many illustrations in this book are from the collection of Christian and Françoise Lacroix. Other sources of illustrations are as follows:

Courtesy Apollo Theatre, London, 82–83 (*main picture*); Collection of the Arles Museums: 40; *Dictionnaire pittoresque de la France*, Arthaud, 1955: 142–143 (*background*); Cecil Beaton Archives, Victoria and Albert Museum, London: 81, 82–83 (*top*), 84 (*bottom*); British Film Institute Stills, Posters and Designs: 110 (*top*), 162 (*left, top to bottom*), 170 (*top right*); Courtesy British Museum: 156 (*second from top*), 157 (*far right bottom*); Courtesy Michel Bonterre: 57; Copyright the Charleston Trust: 102 (*bottom*); Courtesy of Zelda Cheatle Gallery: 84 (*top*), 85; Courtesy Clarkson Potter Inc. *Italian Country Living*, photos Guy Bouchet: 110–111 (*main picture, top right*); *Japanese Style* by Suzanne Slesin, Stafford Cliff and Daniel Rozensztroch, photo Gilles de Chabaneix: 110 (*bottom left*); Photos Lucien Clergue: 137 (*top*), 169 (*top right*); Photograph by Cecil Beaton, by permission of the Condé Nast

Publications Limited; 154 (*left*); Courtesy Wallace Collection, London: 160 (*top left*); Collection Major L. M. E. Dent, D.S.O.: 157 (*bottom left*); Courtesy Dundee Art Galleries and Museum: 168 (*top centre*); Estudios Hareton, Seville: 158 (*top*); Fretz & Wasmuth, AG Zurich, photos Otto Pfeiffer: 34 (*bottom left*), 142 (*centre*), 143 (*bottom right*); Photos Dominique Genet: 1 (*background, inset*), 36 (*background*), 37 (*background*), 40 (*background*), 66–67, 72 (*inset*), 81 (*background*), 84 (*background*), 88, 98–99, 100 (*background, inset*) 102 (*centre*), 103 (*background*), 105 (*top right, bottom right*), 112, 128, 137 (*background*), 139 (*background*), 143 (*top right*), 144 (*background*), 154–155 (*centre*), 159 (*bottom left, bottom right*), 164 (*background*), 168 (*background*); Louvre, Paris, photo Giraudon: 155 (*top*); Courtesy *Harper's Bazaar*, photo Henri Cartier-Bresson: 138 (*top*); Kroller-Müller State Museum, Otterlo: 36 (*centre*); Photo Lafosse/Sygma: 37; Photo Massimo Listri: 159 (*main picture*); Courtesy London Museum: 156 (*bottom left*); Courtesy Maison de Pierre Loti, Rochefort: 107 (*inset bottom left*); Photos Niall McInerney: 155 (*bottom right*), 156 (*top left, second from bottom, bottom second from left*), 157 (*bottom centre*); 164 (*main picture*), 165, 168 (*top left*), 169 (*main picture*); Courtesy National Gallery, London: 160 (*right*); R. Porte, photo Châteaurenard: 34 (*top left*); Courtesy Scala: 108–109; Painting of Lola Montez, by J. Stiegler, courtesy Schloss Nymphenburg, Munich: 171 (*centre right*); Photos Edwin Smith: 106 (*top*), 107 (*inset centre*); Courtesy of Lord Snowdon: 85 (*border*); Courtesy Stilograph, Paris: 103 (*inset*), 104–105; Thames and Hudson Archives: 86–87.

INDEX

Page numbers in *italic* refer to the
illustrations and captions

190

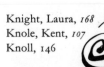